GOODNIGHT, GOD BLESS AND SAFE HOME

FINBAR O'KEEFE, a product of the Irish Army School of Music, grew and blossomed with the showband era and became an integral part of the showband scene from the outset. He toured Ireland with the musically gifted Saints showband, performing on trumpet, guitar and vocals, and appearing on RTE's hour-long TV spectacular, 'The Showband Show'. The band had several successful tours of Great Britain, Germany and the USA. Finbar then exported his talents to England, where he played with New City Sounds before establishing the very successful Las Vegas showband, playing venues as varied as the aircraft carrier HMS Eagle, the Grosvenor House Hotel in London's Park Lane, and at numerous Hunt Balls, Universities and US Air Force bases. He also had a long run on Hughie Green's famous TV talent show, 'Opportunity Knocks'. He is today in a unique position to chronicle the rise, success and demise of the showband on both sides of the water.

GOODNIGHT GOD BLESS

and

SAFE HOME

Finbar O'Keefe

THE O'BRIEN PRESS
DUBLIN

First published 2002 by The O'Brien Press Ltd,
20 Victoria Road, Dublin 6, Ireland.
Tel: +353 1 4923333; Fax: +353 1 4922777
E-mail: books@obrien.ie
Website: www.obrien.ie

ISBN: 0-86278-777-7

British Library Cataloguing-in-Publication Data
O'Keefe, Finbar
Goodnight, God bless and safe home : The golden showband era
1.Big bands - Ireland - History
I.Title
784.1'64'09417'09046

1 2 3 4 5 6
02 03 04 05 06 07

The O'Brien Press receives assistance from

Editing, typesetting, layout and design: The O'Brien Press Ltd

Cover photograph courtesy of Declan Ryan
Printing: Leinster Leader
Picture credits: Mike Gilligan: pp. 25, 84; Syd Shine: p.28; Brendan Bowyer: p.49;
Michael O'Reilly: p.52; George Jones: p.53; Peter McDonald: p.54; Joe Flynn: pp. 60, 82; Keith Donald:
p.128; Donal Gallagher: p.95; Declan Ryan: pp. 97, 144: Frankie McDonald: p.115; Doc Carroll: p.125
Reproductions of *Spotlight* magazine photos and pages by
kind permission of John Coughlan.
Extract from Van Morrison interview by permission of *Hot Press* magazine.
For further information on Van Morrison see
www.hotpress.com

Dedication

The intention of this book is not to create yet another directory of the showbands, as the history of the pacesetters is already well known and very well recorded. This is intended to be a personal view of the overall scene – from both sides of the bandstand and both sides of the water, memory lapses and all. As not every musician was lucky enough to make it into the few headline bands, it tries not to omit the 'engine' of the whole business – the average working band – who also had a part to play and a story to tell. This book is dedicated to all those splendid fellow musicians, drivers, managers and promoters who contributed or were part of the showband scene in any way. It is also dedicated, with my heartfelt thanks, to those hundreds of thousands of dancers, the length and breadth of Ireland, without whom it could never have happened. They were the most important ingredient in what became known and what we fondly recall today as 'The Showband Years'. Thank you all for helping to make that golden era as enjoyable, exciting, entertaining, rewarding and memorable as it certainly was.

Acknowledgements

Many people have helped me put this book together. I would like to thank all my former showband colleagues and others who were so helpful with encouragement, quotes, memories, and with photographs:

Brendan Bowyer (Royal), Doc Carroll (Royal Blues), Seamus Casey (Manager, Joe Dolan), John Coughlan (Spotlight Magazine), Paddy Cole (Capitol), Ronan Collins, RTÉ, Joe Dolan and Ben Dolan (Drifters), Keith Donald (Real McCoy), Joe Flynn (Saints and Showcase), Donal Gallagher, Mike Gilligan (Royal), Frankie McDonald (Drifters), Keith McDonald, The Showband Show, Brendan O'Brien (Dixies), Eileen Reed (Cadets), former Taoiseach Albert Reynolds, Dickie Rock (Miami), Pat Rock, Shannonside Northern Sound FM, Declan Ryan (Regal Showband), Syd Shine (Saints), Gene Turbett (Melody Aces), John Waters, The Irish Times. My love and gratitude to my wife Diane, for her unfailing support and patience, and to my daughter and son Kerri and Ryan for their encouragement and inspiration.

I'd also like to thank the very talented team at The O'Brien Press, especially my editor Mary Webb for her keen insight, professionalism, patience and help – and humour, and also Emma Byrne who, despite all the problems I gave her, still achieved this excellent design and layout.

Contents

Foreword

The late 'fifties and early 'sixties – a simple and uncomplicated time, a time of optimism, of hope, change and dreams. Was it that we were younger then, more innocent, or just more easily pleased? I spent most of that time in Athlone, home base to the army's Western Command Band, which I had joined in 1956 and where I served until 1963. Then, as now, the army band was a nursery for musical talent, producing and honing the skills of musicians who would one day grace the stages of ballrooms throughout the country.

As a young bandsman I little realised what an impact music was to make on my later life. It was to open so many doors, trigger so many experiences, harvest so many memories and allow me to meet so many people I would never have had the chance to meet otherwise. It was also to deprive me of much regular sleep and subject me to more than my fair quota of secondary or passive smoking in the blue haze of the nation's dance halls in later years.

On leaving the army I was fortunate enough to become part of a showband called (in hindsight not very aptly) the Saints, and share in the incredible experience that was the showband scene in Ireland. The sun seemed always to shine then and every bend on the endless road brought another town, another venue, another experience to top up our now golden store of memories. It was hard work but enjoyable and very rewarding. I have an indelible recollection of the time, of the places and more especially of my friends and fellow band-members. When I set out to write this book, the memories came flooding back – of the dances and dancers, the songs, the rehearsals, the camaraderie of the bandwagon. A bond was forged then which still exists strongly to this day. We did not have much money but, by God, we were rich – in health, hopes, talent, versatility – and showmanship. That was our forte.

The showband was an academy all of its own. You turned out smartly, cleanly, punctually and uniformly. On stage you had to project, to sell yourself – and in so doing sell the band. That sort of grounding is what honed and groomed the Saints into the outfit we were and earned us the right to stand with the best at that time. That apprenticeship was unique and has been repaid a thousandfold down the years. We have all – including the audiences – been the richer for the experience. Even today, wherever music is played, the 'showband-schooled' musician still stands out – instantly recognisable in any company – and that has to be the showband era's greatest legacy. I am proud to have been a very small part of it.

Here I am, middle right, with the Saints.

The Saints — Athlone
THLONE P.W.
Phone 2113

1. You Blow a Balloon, You Play a Trumpet!

In 1954, at the age of fifteen, I had an interview in the band room at Collins Barracks, Cork, with the then bandmaster, Lieutenant 'Bonnie' Keely. My enthusiasm was initially dampened when the first thing I saw was the bandsmen scrubbing the timber floor, but the sight of the gleaming silver musical instruments soon perked me up. Things went well and three days later, armed with a travel warrant courtesy of the Minister for Defence, a £1 note and wearing my first new long trousers, I caught the Dublin train to what was then Kingsbridge, now Heuston Station, with literally 'everything to play for'.

I was met at the station by a young bandboy and taken to the Army School of Music at Cathal Brugha Barracks. Things were frugal, very firm but also very fair. Lights out was strictly enforced at 10.30pm. The training was intense and varied, with drilling and marching, sports and schooling. The emphasis was clearly on music of the military and classical kinds. It was several weeks before any musical instruments were handed out and then it was very much a game of chance as to what you ended up with. Almost everone had a preference for a saxophone or a trumpet, and I was lucky enough to be handed a trumpet. The lads who were given a tuba or bassoon were visibly disappointed, but these same people went on to become very competent musicians, attached and dedicated to their instruments. I suppose in hindsight the authorities had to foresee the demands of the four army bands and ensure that the right instrumental replacements were in the pipeline as seasoned personnel were due to leave or retire.

Among our group there were some naturally gifted musicians to whom everything appeared to come easily,

but personally, while I was happy with the rudimentary and theory side of the music, I found the performance side very hard going and had to really work at it. I recall looking over some new piece of music at practice one day, holding the trumpet and making the remark: 'I'm just going to blow this.' I was overheard by the sergeant and told very firmly: 'You blow a balloon. You play a trumpet!'

The pay at the time was all of £1/–/3d per week, and no sooner had we been given it than we were immediately paraded to the

On the ball!
The Army School of Music
basketball team, 1955.

canteen to buy boot polish, Brasso, soap, toothpaste, etc. It was often a struggle to retain the shilling and three pence for the Princess or Stella cinemas in Rathmines. The sixpenny slog up the steps of Nelson's Column on O'Connell Street, or even better, the free museums, were our more usual weekend pastime.

There were future showband stalwarts aplenty in the school of music in my time: Frankie Mc Donald – still playing today with Joe Dolan; Liam Meade, who also joined the Drifters; Freddie Martin, who played with the Pacific; Noel Melia, who joined the Ravens; Tommy Rooney, who played with

Donie Collins; and Vince McInhill, who became better know as Prince Vince of the Kings showband.

The two years rolled happily on and I was eventually deemed competent and posted to the army band in Athlone on 19 March 1956.

Men in uniform! With my fellow bandsman, Jackie McLoughlin (right).

2. Black Suits and Dickey Bows: The Sitting-Down Band

'It is arguable that Big Tom was more central to the modernisation of Irish society than the First Programme for Economic Expansion.'
John Waters, The Irish Times, 22 April, 2002

The 'good old days' in the Ireland of the 1950s were, in fact, not very good at all. In reality, Ireland was a drab and stagnant place, still suffering some of the privations and rationing of the war. The country was poor. Employment was at an all time low. Emigration was rife and the mailboat out of Dublin and the MV *Innisfallen* out of Cork were always crowded. Sadly, for far too many the boat fare of £3.10s was the price of a one-way ticket to hope. For those left at home, life went on in the same old grey way. 'Prayers and porter' was author Frank O'Connor's description of rural Ireland at that time. Nothing seemed to change, and this was equally true of the music scene – what there was of one.

There were a few dozen established orchestras who shared the vast majority of dance-band engagements at the time, including: Mick Delahunty, Jack Flahive, The Regal Dance Orchestra, Des Fretwell, Maurice Mulcahy, Jack Ruane, Gay McEntyre, Brose Walsh, Syd Shine and his Crescent Dance Orchestra. They were all household names who enjoyed an unassailable position in a time that had no competition to offer. Alternative forms of entertainment were scarce. Cinemas were few and far between and usually showed the same film for a full week. There was no television, no video, no bingo halls or bowling alleys, and most definitely no discos or karaoke. What musical entertainment there was, was provided by 'the wireless', which in some rural houses was switched on only for the All-Ireland finals, the news or 'Take the Floor'. Today's generation finds it hilarious and unbelievable that households throughout Ireland avidly tuned in to Raidio Éireann to listen to Irish dancing. But we did, and there would be much comment afterwards on the wonderful footwork of the Rory O'Connor champion dancers! Is it any wonder that the 'live' entertainment provided by the sober-suited dance bands was so popular?

The professional dance bands boasted between ten and eighteen musicians. On stage they sat down and read their music parts from arranged orchestration sheets on music stands in front of them. As each new song was issued it would be numbered by the band members and, as the dances were played in sets of three tunes each, the bandleader would simply call out, for example, 'forty-one, twenty-three, thirty-seven,' and the next three numbers would be played in that order .

It was a bit like ordering from a Chinese takeaway!

The Davitt Brothers band, from Ferns. Yes, they really are all brothers!

The dances were very formal affairs and, while the musical sound was often superb, the black-attired bands, sitting down, foraging through their music libraries for the next numbers, could not and did not offer too much in the way of excitement, dynamism or colour.

Then there were the 'semi-pro' dance bands, who provided me, and many other future showband musicians, with an invaluable musical education. As my army day officially finished at 4.30pm (barring any special parades, funerals or band engagements), I decided to take up a 'sideline career' in my spare time. This was not frowned on as long as it did not interfere with official army band duties. My introduction to the dance-band world of the time was through playing with such notables as the 'Bullet' Dempsey, Jack Beahan and JJ Carr (the very names still conjure up reverence and awe in the music fraternity). I remember how JJ would pick up anyone passing by with a musical instrument to augment the band, with the comment, 'There's safety in numbers.' I was initially viewed with great suspicion for carrying a guitar, as this was, even at that early stage, rightly viewed as a direct threat to the orchestra-style bands.

The Bullet Dempsey was notorious for his late arrivals at venues. He would attempt to placate the irate parish priest with a most colourful tale of an overheated engine and not one, but two punctures. His 'two punctures' story was a classic. It became so common and expected that finally he would just say 'Father', and hold up the two fingers. Then he would add, 'But sure Father, we're worth waitin' for.' As a young, raw, green bandsman it was a priceless grounding for which I have always remained grateful. But, while it was very enjoyable, it was unbelievably amateurish by today's standards.

The entire band, plus all their equipment, piled into one car and travelled to the gig already attired in their stage dress – black suits and dickey bows – no matter how far away the gig was or how long the journey. The dances were normally held in church-controlled parish halls and, knowing that there was no chance of a drink there, the main topic of discussion on the way centred on the best route to take in order to acquire the necessary 'liquid refreshment'. Any old pub wouldn't do; most bands had a particular favourite and a detour of twenty miles was not uncommon to include this in the itinerary. There was a very practical reason for this lunacy: In those far-off days, most pubs charged a ha'penny on each bottle of Guinness taken out, and as the required quota was generally three crates, it was worth the extra distance if the bottle charge could be waived, hence the favourite pubs. Of course, part of the deal required that the empties be returned in the early hours

QUAY ROAD HALL
BALLYCASTLE

Dancing to Ireland's Top
Showbands
EVERY FRIDAY NIGHT

on the way home, when the pub would conveniently be open to receive them, and when invariably the band's fee for the night ended up in the pub till! Sounds far-fetched, but I assure you it's true.

The musicians then were wonderfully uncomplicated people, who had their priorities right and did not take themselves, punctuality or life too seriously, so I was quick to learn that a pick-up time of 5.30pm really meant seven o'clock. The payout came as you left the car at the barrack gate in the early hours, when a note was squeezed into your hand – always under cover of darkness so you could not distinguish what denomination it was – and always with the consoling words: 'Sure, 'tis great experience for you.' The paper money invariably proved to be the old orange ten-shilling note but, despite the paltry pay, it was great experience and I would already be looking forward to the next gig.

You were required to apply for and carry a signed late pass each time you were unlikely to make the 1am curfew, which of course, was every time you had an outside gig. As you entered the barrack gate, tired and vulnerable at 5am, when all sensible people had most of their night's sleep already over, the military policeman on duty would decide to have some fun at your expense. One in particular, a great character called 'Mugser' Kelly, would inform you, with great urgency and sincerity, that the President was visiting and that parade was at 8am. Panicked, you spent the next two hours shining and polishing, and ensuring your dress uniform was spick and span, only to find out that there was no presidential visit and no dress uniform parade. I was gullible in those days.

There was the occasional but inevitable clash of dates, when an official army engagement coincided with a dance-band booking. I recall band leaders waiting in panic at the barrack gate, hoping that the next bus to turn the corner would be the coach returning us from the Spring Show or the Horse Show in the RDS in Ballsbridge, and then having to hold their tempers while we were ordered to 'Fall Out' and made a mad scramble to change from uniform to our dance civvies.

There were some large, established dance halls (we did not call them ballrooms in those days), and many hotels had function rooms for dancing, but most local dances were held in parish halls. These were drab places, purely functional, sparse and often cold. They were multi-functional, being used for concerts, plays by local drama groups and community activities. If you looked closely at the dance floor, you could often see the lines where it was marked out for basketball and other indoor sports. The dressing rooms – if they had any – were, for some inexplicable reason, always piled high with chairs or tables. Fortunately, as we were already wearing our band suits, we did not need to use them. A meal was normally provided for us at an adjacent house, and it was always the same: sliced ham and tomatoes. After travelling a hundred miles and being a growing lad, I was ready and grateful for it. If it was good enough for them it was good enough for me. On occasion a good-hearted committee would provide a crate of Guinness for the band; this would be locked in the dressing room cupboard, the key of which was jealously guarded by some go-fer. He would tell us a hundred times that there was a drink for the band, that he had got the key but could not open the cupboard until after the dance was finished. We solved this dilemma by carrying a screwdriver and unscrewing the door hinges. When he finally opened up and was confronted with empty bottles there would be a lot of explaining to do.

The dances were very parochial affairs, where everyone knew not just the person they were dancing with, but their fa-ther and mother, brothers and sisters as well. The presence of a stranger was the subject of great discussion, conjecture and gossip. The parish priest was often in attendance to oversee the event and I am told that the convent-educated girls would already have been warned by the nuns to 'leave room for the Holy Ghost', in other words, to keep a respectable dis-tance between themselves and their partners. What killjoys! Alcohol was also taboo in the dance halls, and whatever about the quantity that might have been consumed by the lads be-fore they came in, the only refreshments inside were cups of tea or bottles of minerals. These 'dry', supervised dances were practically the sole form of enter-tainment for Ireland's young – and not so young – apart from the cinema, or 'picture house' as they were known then.

The first real indication that there were other things happening music-wise out there in the larger world was the Top Twenty broadcast

The electric guitar – a frightening sight for a sitting-down band.

by Radio Luxembourg –'The Station of the Stars' – on 208 on the medium wave. It aired on Sunday nights from 10pm to twelve midnight and became required listening for those with the means to tune in to it. It created a buzz and excitement that the regulated and strictly controlled youngsters of Ireland, of whom I was one, wanted to be part of.

Change was in the air. The natives were getting restless. With the war now long over, austerity was at last on the wane and the holidaying Irish home from England – having seen 'the lights' – began to say, 'Entertain me.' The young people of Ireland, who for centuries had 'known their place' and obeyed the stricture to be 'seen and not heard', began to stir. They were no longer content to meekly accept whatever was on offer. Up to now they had had no authentic sound or collective identity that they could relate to or call their own, but that was about to change. In the dance-band world, things would never again be the same.

3. Enter the Showband: Mohair and Magic

'The showband era was a most wonderful and exciting time for me and all the boys in the band and I don't think the exhilaration of that revolutionary time will ever be emulated.'
Dickie Rock, the Miami showband

I t is generally accepted that the pathfinders were the Clipper Carlton, a band hailing from Strabane in Northern Ireland and featuring the now legendary names of Hugo Quinn, Hugh Tourish and Fergie O'Hagan. By the mid-1950s, the Clippers had swept away their music stands, added variety and comedy to their musical programme and began to 'sell' and project their show. Thus began the revolutionary era of the showbands. The Clipper Carlton introduced a twenty-minute cabaret spot – called 'Juke Box Saturday Night' – in which they 'took off' the hit bands of

The Clipper Carlton

the time. It was hugely popular and the effect on the audience was startling. Dancers suddenly came to a halt and crowded round the stage to watch, wonder and applaud. This was a major culture shock for the Irish punters of that time, who had come expecting the usual restrictive and staid diet of three quicksteps, three waltzes and three foxtrots. The word 'showstopper' was coined for these tunes.

After fourteen years playing together, the Clippers were suddenly an overnight sensation. Make no mistake, these people had always been very accomplished musically, but what had changed was the format. Whereas before, dance bands had simply sat down and played from their music sheets, this band now also entertained; it was revolutionary, vibrant, alive, energetic and very different. I was totally hooked when I first saw the Clippers play at the Sportex Hall in Athlone. What struck me most was the freedom, the movement and the sheer enjoyment they appeared to experience; somehow it all looked so natural. I can clearly remember the discussions in the army bandroom the following morning (usually the talk was about girls) as some of us tried to remember and rehearse the step routines. You can imagine the comments of our watching colleagues, or then again maybe you can't!

There is no doubt that what the Clipper Carlton started lit the fuse that ignited the showband explosion of the 'sixties. The word soon spread and it was now very much 'catch-up time' for any band intending to stay in the business. The change was gradual rather than instant, as it took time for bands to alter

**Two great showband veterans.
Left: Earl Gill, trumpeter with the Hoedowners.
Below: ex-Saint Frankie McDonald, still playing with
Joe Dolan's band.**

their set programmes and stage presentation, but once started, there was no turning back.

There were other changes too – gone was the formal black dress suit; in came bright red or blue jackets, stripes, white trousers, white shoes, even hats in some cases. There was colour, variety and movement. The whole band moved in unison to the music in coordinated steps that had been perfected at rehearsal. In the better bands the steps – probably modelled on the famous 'Shadow steps' created by Cliff Richard and the Shadows – became second nature. Soon, kicks were being added to coincide with a particular cymbal crash or a rimshot beat and it was always visually impressive to see seven or eight lads on stage kick out simultaneously at exactly the right moment. I remember feeling a bit self-conscious the first few times we did our 'performance' but it soon became great fun and definitely added to the show.

Bass guitars, unheard of until then, began to replace the large and familiar double bass, allowing much more freedom of movement and providing a more modern sound – not to mention the convenience of being more easily transportable. Have you ever driven from Athlone, County Westmeath, to Roundstone in Connemara in a Zephyr 4 with seven passengers inside and a double bass strapped to the roof? I have. It was purgatory, but the stuff of legends and all part of the apprenticeship.

Another fundamental requirement of the new set-up was the inclusion of a brass section – generally trumpet, tenor sax and trombone – giving the showband its unique and instantly recognisable sound. The brass arrangements were so effective that the 'riffs' in showband standards like 'Old Man Trouble', 'Yesterday Man', 'Ring of Fire', 'Baby I'm your Man' and 'Make Me an Island' were as familiar and recognisable to the dancers as the songs themselves. Something that is much commented on now, but was never raised at the time, was the fact that the showbands' repertoire consisted almost 100 percent of 'cover' versions of the pop songs of the day. No one was complaining; they played them brilliantly and they sold them brilliantly, and the dancers came back for more, again and again. I can't recall hearing an original tune until much later on in the showbands' reign.

Few of those coming to a marquee to hear a showband will ever forget the sound that greeted them through the canvas as they approached. It was fresh, it was bright and it was punchy – a magical combination. The overall effect was captivating, unforgettable and addictive. Chairs on the bandstand were now becoming a distant memory and the first question a new band enquiring for a booking was asked was, 'Are ye a standin' up or a sittin' down band?' To that question there was now only one right answer.

4. Cars and Vans and Hearses: Transports of Delight

'My family always believed that I would become a medical Doc[tor], but they could never have believed that I would become a "Rockin' Doc", which I did, thanks to the showbands.'
Doc Carroll, the Royal Blues

Private jets and stretch limos may be commonplace to today's musicians, but four wheels – any four wheels – were the transport of the very early bands, and if you had an engine that wasn't on its last legs you were lucky.

Loading up was an art form. The unfortunates occupying the rear seat had to squeeze in first and the excess equipment was then loaded onto their knees for the duration of what could be a very long journey. Consequently there was a strict rota to occupy the old front bench seats which were the norm in cars at the time.

Syd and the Saints, with bandwagon, outside the Crescent ballroom, Athlone.

When you hear nowadays of deep vein thrombosis being brought on by cramped seating on airlines, it is a wonder that we survived at all, never mind going on to present a couple of hours of synchronised dance stepping!

I remember several occasions in very rural areas where we had to use the car battery to power the PA system for the duration of the dance. By the end of the night the battery would be drained and some hefty pushing by the band would be required to bring the engine back to life for the journey homeward. For a short time I played with a band where we used a local hackney driver who was paid as an extra band member, so if the gig was very local he was well 'in pocket', but if it was sixty miles away he didn't do so well. He normally slept in the car while we played – a cushy number!

Band transport evolved in line with the growth of the business. As the showbands evolved, with their eight-piece line-ups and bigger and extra equipment, the car was abandoned and a bandwagon of some sort had to be acquired. The purpose-built bandwagon had not yet made an appearance and the early 'wagons' came in all shapes and sizes, from bread vans to old Post Office vans and ambulances. Chip vans were converted and even a retired hearse was brought into service, but the early favourites were the Volkswagen minibus and the Commer van. Reliability was crucial, so maintenance was always a priority. The long hours travelling meant that the wagon was a 'second home', so every effort went into making it as comfortable as possible. Some musicians proved amazingly skilled at DIY, fitting coach or aircraft seats, putting

Before the goldrush – the VW bandwagon of the Royal showband.

up shelving and built-in wardrobes for the band's stage outfits, which were no longer worn on the journey.

I have also experienced wagons that were cold and draughty, in which, when the heater failed on a winter's night, you had to sit shivering and huddled together for three to four hours on the trip home. Apart from getting you to the show and back, the wagon also became a very important advertising vehicle and it was customary to display the band's name prominently on both sides as well as the back, with contact numbers for anyone who might be a potential booker. Some bands had their name in a display light, which was mounted on top of the cab and flashed on and off. This caused problems on English tours, where only emergency vehicles such as police, fire engines or ambulances were allowed to display rooftop lights. Many of the Irish bands were pulled over and cautioned.

In my view, the bandwagon played a pivotal role in the life and success of the showbands. It bonded the band together, it became the place where most of the better ideas were hatched, and it was generally the place where major band decisions were discussed and taken, principally because the whole band was in attendance and on a long journey there was the time for discussion with very few distractions.

The rear third of the van was generally partitioned off, and this area was used to carry the band gear. One of the band members was normally nominated as loadmaster and, after the gig, the gear was ferried out to him. His job was to load and unload the wagon in a particular order, as every item had its own specific place. This was important, as it made it easier to check if an item was missing. After a long gig in Kilfinane or Bruree he could say, just by glancing in at what seemed to me to be a mountain of miscellaneous gear, 'I'm missing the clarinet,' or, 'I need another mike stand.' It was also amazing just how much he could actually fit in. Instruments were very personal items and very much treasured by their owners so the more compact ones, such as trumpets, were often carried inside the wagon by the owner.

For the more successful bands, the Mercedes coach was the ultimate 'must have' vehicle and it quickly became a status symbol. At every gig it would be strategically parked, normally outside the ballroom box office where the queueing punters had plenty of opportunity to see it. It was always a great point of discussion and of course was also a very strong and direct advert for the band and the ballroom, as it declared loudly who was playing at the venue, and how well they were doing. Of course, if your wagon was a rust box it was parked well out of sight! I recall seeing some full-size passenger buses which had been fitted with sleeping bunks, curtains and washstands, etc., but I felt this was a bit over the top; it was changing the whole role of the bandwagon, and running costs, parking and manoeuvrability would have been questionable.

I am of the personal opinion that when bands started to use their own cars to get to and from gigs, a very important ingredient was lost from the successful showband formula.

5. Becoming a Saint

The Crescent ballroom in Athlone was a well established and very popular dance venue in the 'fifties. It was owned and run by Syd Shine, a local businessman and a musician of note. Syd fronted the ten-piece Crescent Dance Orchestra, the resident band in the ballroom every Thursday and Sunday night, who had established a reputation for their tempo, quality and musicianship. This was hardly surprising, as the band was mostly comprised of members

The Crescent ballroom, Athlone. The area behind the railings was known as 'the Corral'.

The Saints, minus two.

of the army band of the Western Command, who were stationed in Athlone.

Positions in the dance band were jealously guarded as it was considered a 'plum' job, with regular local bookings and not too much travelling. They also played many prestigious engagements, including, on several occasions, the much sought-after Trinity Ball in Dublin. Syd's band always seemed to have the extra few quid. You can imagine the rest of us army bandsmen eagerly queuing up when a vacancy arose, which was all too rarely.

However, time rolled on and, in 1962, even the popular Crescent ballroom could not withstand the musical wind of change that was blowing through Ireland. The decision was taken to replace the orchestra with a five-piece group that would still cover the two nights' residency and also cater for hotel functions: dinner dances, candlelight dinners and so on. One Saturday morning I was approached by Joe Flynn, the bass guitar player, in the army band room. Joe outlined to me the advantages of the two-nights-a-week local residency, reminded me of Syd Shine's contacts in the business and then played his trump card: there would be a retainer of £10 a week, even if we had no gig at all. I was convinced. I joined the new group on guitar, trumpet and vocals. Syd was the bandleader and we played under the name Syd and the Saints.

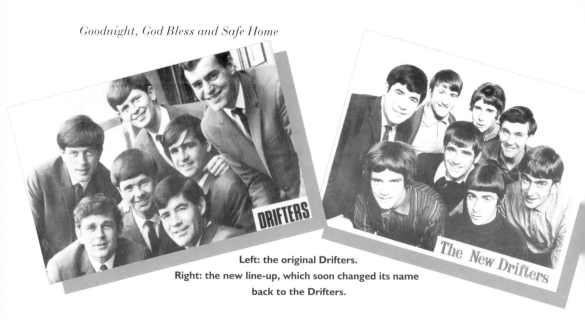

**Left: the original Drifters.
Right: the new line-up, which soon changed its name
back to the Drifters.**

It quickly became apparent at rehearsals that the smaller the line-up, the more dependable you have to become. You have to contribute in any band, but in a big band it is possible to 'carry' individuals, something that is just not workable with a five-piece. The contribution had to be 100 percent and you were under constant assessment, but it did lead to a considerable improvement in performance. The line-up also included Frank Somers on drums and Pete Keighery on lead guitar and vocals. I am happy to report that Frank is still playing today, with Foster and Allen, and Joe Flynn fronts the popular Showcase, a four-piece group who specialise in ballroom dancing in venues such as Jury's Hotel, Dublin. He has appeared on 'The Late Late Show' and 'Open House'. Pete is now Customer Services Manager with Carr Golf in Dublin (nice work if you can get it).

The new band had a great year and in 1963 I bought myself out of the army band, at a cost of £200. The showband boom was by now in full swing. Our five-piece was not big enough to be accepted in the new ballrooms that were being built, so we decided to augment the band to a full showband line-up of eight. I put forward the names of three of the army bandsmen I had known and whose abilities I could vouch for. The first two were Liam Meade (Trombone/Vocals) and Frankie McDonald (Trumpet/Vocals). Both were later to join Joe Dolan and the Drifters following the departure of Tommy and Jimmy Swarbrigg. The final target was Brian Sullivan, a young, dynamic vocalist and frontman who also played tenor saxophone. Unfortunately, the army band and my three pals were serving with the UN in Cyprus at the time, but I managed to contact them and give them the sales pitch, and on their return they signed up with the band. The Saints showband was born. The new personnel made an immediate impact – the sound was much fuller, and on stage the band looked and sounded more balanced. I remember feeling more relaxed playing with the enlarged line-up, as there was not the same pressure and there were more vocalists to share the workload. We were averaging about four bookings a week, at venues in all corners of the country.

The band had standards and style, and if you wanted to be part of it you had to measure up. In its outlook, the Saints was as professional as any of the professional bands of the time. Numbers were not just tunes to be played, they were 'productions' – directed, styled and choreographed. I can hear it now: 'Always step to the left – on the left, but never on the upbeat.' Stops – natural breaks in the tempo of the music – were important and effective when utilised properly. It was essential for presentation that the whole band stopped moving when a 'stop' was reached. If you inadvertently 'ran into a stop', you let the side down and they let you know it. You very soon learned to feel them; you had to.

In a typical week we might play the Ritz in Carlow, the Silver Slipper in Strandhill, the Marine in Enniscrone and the Butt Hall in Ballybofey. The travelling didn't bother us unduly; we were well able for it at that time. Every gig was different and we looked forward to each one. A manager was appointed to look after the affairs of the band, in the person of Pat Noone from Claremorris, County Mayo. Pat did a great job in a very competitive market, and made an effort to personally attend as many gigs as possible. He was also responsible for the UK and USA tours and the 'Showband Show' appearance of the band. While we never achieved a position in the top ten commercially successful showbands, we nevertheless enjoyed great respect within the business and, on reflection, we really had great fun. We did not have the pressures of the headline bands and therefore had the time to draw breath, to look around and to enjoy the whole scene. We experienced the excitement of the time and the musical revolution at first hand, and took all that was good from it into our future musical ventures. There is no doubt that it has served us well.

6. A Right Royal Time: The Showband Boom

'I was studying architecture in London when the Dixies went pro. I joined the band intending to stay for one year, but when the money began rolling in, the one year turned into forty and the architecture was forgotten.'

Brendan O'Brien, the Dixies showband

Up and down the country, the length and breadth of Ireland, showbands began to emerge, grow and prosper. From Waterford came the Royal, the Savoy, the Blue Aces; Cork produced the Victors, the Dixies, the Regal; from Kilkenny came the Black Aces; Mullingar produced the Drifters; Limerick had the Monarchs and Donie Collins; Dublin provided the Miami, the Cadets, the Pacific, the Capitol, the Nevada; from Mayo came Doc Carroll and the Royal Blues and Jack Ruane; Strabane was home to the Clipper Carlton; Derry had Johnny Quigley; the Melody Aces and the Platter-men hailed from Omagh; Ballymena had the Freshmen; the Swingtime Aces came from Athenry; Johnny Flynn hailed from Tuam, County Galway. The list goes on: six, maybe seven hundred in total when the showbands' popularity was at its height.

The Capitol: always among the top ten bands. Butch Moore is centre, with Paddy Cole far left.

There was a great rapport between the bands as they criss-crossed the country. A rivalry, yes, but a mutual respect also, as they all strived for success. It was hard work, involving long hours and constant travelling, but for the lucky ones who made it the financial rewards were fabulous. While the average national wage in 1960 was £9/£10 per week, the bigger showbands at their peak were commanding £600–£700 per night. It was almost always in cash; I have heard stories of suitcases full of notes in hotel rooms.

The money, the success, and the fame: it was a lot to handle. Many showband members were lads from some country town or village, and the environment into which they were thrust so suddenly was completely alien to them. It has to be said that the majority of them lived their new life to the full. The ham and tomato meals of the early days were now replaced by fillet steaks and mixed grills with all the trimmings. In some of the more successful bands, the bandwagon – that communal home, card club, after-gig ideas forum, and team builder – was discarded in favour of the personal motorcar. This created its own problems, not least because it greatly increased the potential for car

The Royal Blues, with Doc Carroll. This is *not* their bandwagon!

ROYAL SHOWBAND

accidents,
of which there were quite   a few,
some sadly resulting in the deaths of
band members. I can well remember
playing at Hayden's Hotel in Ballinasloe
one night and admiring a row of flashy

Prized autographs of the most popular band in the country.

imported cars parked outside; it transpired that they belonged to the lads in
the Royal Blues who were playing locally – they had bought one each.

But with the big money came pitfalls for the unwary. There were endless
hours of travel to, and then home from, the gigs. There was broken, intermit-
tent, irregular sleep. There were boring, wet, winter days spent hanging around
in hotels, with alcohol beckoning and helpful barmen only too eager to be of
service. It took a fairly strong character to cope with that sort of temptation,
and unfortunately not everyone did. Although in many of the early showband
photos it was common to see members sporting Pioneer pins, later on alcohol
ruined many a musical career, and sometimes marriages and families as well.

You were not permitted to fall ill if you were a showband member. Like
most others, I have had to turn up, switch on the smile and perform the steps
while suffering from a raging flu or other bug. It was expected. An additional

REGAL SHOWBAND, CORK

THE WITNESSES BANDSHOW

Be Your Own Judge

and unpleasant complication for every brass-man was the dreaded cold sore, which always appeared right on the embouchure where your lip met the mouthpiece and caused agony when trying to blow normally. Still, the show must go on.

The Royal would have to be considered the most successful of the show-bands. They evolved from a local Waterford band called the Harry Boland Dance Band, when an impressed musical instrument salesman, TJ Byrne, became their manager. As happens in all the best scripts, he changed their name and within weeks they became, and stayed, the 'hottest ticket' nationwide on the showband circuit. They packed ballrooms all over the country and became the first show-band to make a record: the late Tom Dunphy's 'Come Down the Mountain, Katie Daly'. The Royal notched up an unbelievable eight number one smash hits in the Irish charts, including, of course, Brendan Bowyer's leg-endary 'Hucklebuck', which was originally intended as the B-side of their new record and was recorded in a remarkable twenty minutes! It spent twelve weeks in the Irish charts and was at number one for seven of those. Other hits for Brendan included

THE MIGHTY AVONS

'Kiss Me Quick', 'No More', 'Bless You', and 'Don't Lose Your Hucklebuck Shoes'. Tom Dunphy chipped in with another number one, 'If I Didn't Have a Dime'. Charlie Mathews, not to be outdone, climbed to the top with 'Somewhere My Love', while Jim Conlon also topped the charts with his guitar theme from the band's film, *The One-Nighters*. To cap it all, they were the only Irish showband to win the coveted Carl Allen award for record box-office attendances in the British dance halls. Las Vegas was to beckon and the rest, as they say, is history.

My favourite personal memory of the Royal showband is from one night around 1965 when the Saints and myself were playing in the Greville Arms Hotel in Mullingar for the race meeting dinner dance. The Royal had a race-horse – appropriately named Royal Showband – that had won that day, and the boys were celebrating at the function. Inevitably, Brendan was persuaded to join us on stage. He sang a few numbers, one of which was 'Boolavogue', in that great, soaring, powerful voice of his. And if I do say so myself, the backing wasn't too bad either.

Of course, not all of the showbands were stars. Outside of the top dozen or so, there existed several hundred bands desperate to emulate the success of those at the pinnacle. These bands were vital to the success of the whole showband industry. They all had hopes and dreams and these were the guys who put the smiles on the faces of music shop owners, tailors and garages, as they bought the latest guitar or echo chamber, or speakers, in an effort to copy the leaders and try to improve their overall sound, or flashy stage suits to spruce up their image. Many were good, solid bands and did steady work, as the top boys could not play everywhere, but they were certainly not paid anything like the lucrative fees negotiated by the 'stars'. Simple mathematics show that a promoter sometimes made more from a middle-of-the-road band with an average crowd, because of the huge percentages of the takings they had to pay to the top bands. These started out at fifty percent, but the top five showbands could, on special nights, command seventy percent, with a guaranteed fee if the take fell below a certain figure. It was all down to pulling power, demand and astute management. The leading crowd-pullers held all the aces. The promoter dared not risk losing their services or have them playing in another venue in his area, taking his customers with them. So, while he did not like it, he was generally forced to concede to the deal.

There were other hall promoters who would not risk the fees demanded by the top bands, so there was a market for the middle bands. A decent living could be made like this, but the dream was always to join a top showband, for the glamour as much as for the money. Around these headliner bands a whole new peripheral industry was born, grew and blossomed – band gear, PA systems, stage wear, customised transport, recording studios, magazines, posters, free photo handouts, publicity. CIÉ even laid on a 'Johnny Flynn Special' train to take dancers to the Tuam-based showband's venues at the peak of the craze.

A new magazine, *Spotlight*, was launched in Cork in 1963 to cater for the huge interest in the showbands. It became very successful and by the late 'sixties the magazine, now re-named *New Spotlight*, was the biggest-selling music weekly in the country, with a circulation of more than 50,000 copies a week. The magazine chronicled the progress of the bands, reviewed new releases, carried the top twenty chart (which by now had plenty of Irish showband records in it) and also covered the folk and beat scenes. Originally written and produced by John Coughlan, who remained its managing editor until it ceased publication in 1975, the magazine's regular contributors included names that are familiar to everyone in the Irish music scene today, such as Larry Gogan, BP Fallon, Shay Healy and Pat Egan.

★★★★★ **POLL EXTRA** ★★★★★

IRELAND'S TOP BANDS

IRELAND'S top ten bands in 1969 as voted by the country's ballroom owners and dance promoters on the basis of average crowd attendance throughout the year were as follows, in alphabetical order.

DIXIES
DREAMS
DRIFTERS
FRESHMEN
HOEDOWNERS

MIAMI
MAINLINERS & BIG TOM
MIGHTY AVONS
ROYAL
SANDS

NEXT TEN

The next ten, again in alphabetical order were:

CAPITOLS
CADETS
NEVADA
PACIFIC
PLATTERMEN

PREMIER ACES
ROYAL BLUES
SOUNDS
TIMES
VICTORS

★★★★★★★★★★★★★★★★★★★★★★★★

Ireland's top bands, according to a Spotlight magazine poll in 1969.

7. Breeze-block Basilicas:
The Ballroom Revolution

'The explosion in the building of ballrooms throughout Ireland in the late 'fifties and 'sixties and the birth and growth of the showband era represented a social revolution and was the forerunner of an extremely successful Irish music industry.'

Albert Reynolds, former taoiseach

As the crowds got bigger and bigger, the parish halls, and even the larger dance halls, were no longer big enough to accommodate the thousands who were prepared to pay good money to see their favourite bands. The construction industry thrived as new and ever-larger ballrooms sprung up all over the country, sometimes in places so remote that you would wonder where the crowd could possibly come from. But come they did, even if it meant travelling for hours to get there.

Among those who saw and seized the opportunity were the Reynolds brothers, Jim and Albert – the latter going on to become a successful politician, achieving 'top billing' in his own right as Taoiseach of Ireland. The Reynolds brothers were largely responsible for dragging the Irish rural dancing culture out of the dark ages. Jim and Albert

Ballroom tycoon turned taoiseach – Albert Reynolds.

marched, rather than tentatively stepped, into their ballroom venture with the opening of the Cloudland ballroom in Rooskey, County Roscommon in September 1957. This proved to be as enlightened as it was brave, as few could have foreseen the coming showband explosion at this early date. Jim was very much the 'hands-on' type, and was physically involved with all aspects of the building projects, while Albert looked after the administration, the publicity, the advertising and the booking of the bands. On the building sites, teams of between fifteen and twenty-five men were employed. Four or five of these were key men who worked on all of the building projects, while the remainder were recruited locally. The plans and layout for each ballroom were very similar, with perhaps a slight change to the frontage. In 1959, the second Reynolds ballroom – the Roseland in Moate, County Westmeath – opened its doors for business. At six o'clock on the first evening they were still hanging those same front doors. Mick Delahunty was booked to open the new venue.

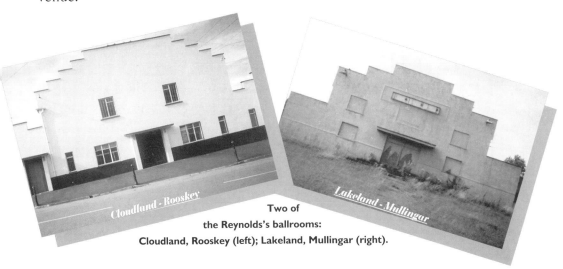

Two of the Reynolds's ballrooms: Cloudland, Rooskey (left); Lakeland, Mullingar (right).

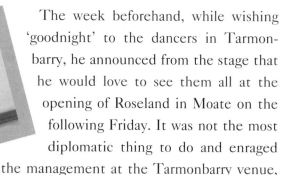

The week beforehand, while wishing 'goodnight' to the dancers in Tarmonbarry, he announced from the stage that he would love to see them all at the opening of Roseland in Moate on the following Friday. It was not the most diplomatic thing to do and enraged the management at the Tarmonbarry venue, who felt that their customers were being poached.

Next came the Fairyland ballroom in Roscommon town, where, as the band pulled up for the opening night, an inside wall of the ballroom was still being plastered, with the painters following along behind. How's that for scheduling? The business was becoming lucrative and, with competitors on the lookout, locations for new ventures were kept hush-hush. So it was that, one night in June 1963, two men came to be inspecting a field on the outskirts of Mullingar, County Westmeath by torchlight. One of these men was Jim Reynolds. A solicitor was instructed and the site was bought the following morning; by 3.30 that same afternoon the diggers had arrived. This was the site for the Lakeland ballroom, Mullingar and it opened in September 1963.

Another Reynolds ballroom, Dreamland in Athy, County Kildare, had the distinction of hosting the Royal showband every St Stephen's night for five consecutive years – a successful bit of business on both sides, one would imagine. The Jetland in Limerick was the biggest ballroom in the Reynolds chain – on one memorable night it packed in a record-breaking 4,125 dancers.

Other ballrooms built by the Reynolds brothers included: Danceland, Portlaoise; Barrowland, New Ross; Rockland, Borris in Ossary; Borderland, Clones; Moyland, Ballina; Hiland, Newmarket; and Wonderland, Cavan.

The main opposition to the Reynolds monopoly came from Associated Ballrooms, an amalgamation of Con Hynes, who had the Las Vegas ballroom in Templemore, County Tipperary; Donie Collins, the bandleader from Askeaton, County Limerick; and Jack O'Rourke, of the Majestic ballroom, Mallow, County Cork.

The owners of the big ballrooms had the power to make or break a band and if these people gave you 'the nod' you were home and dry. The Arcadia in

Bray was recognised as the biggest in the country, with the Majorca in Crosshaven, County Cork – owned by the Lucey brothers and commonly known as 'Crosser' – a close second. Dickie Rock and the Miami played to a crowd of 4,000 there and thirty double-decker buses were required to ferry the dancers from Cork's Grand Parade.

Although we played in most of the dance halls and ballrooms in the country, inevitably, there are one or two memories that stand out. Whenever I hear mention of the Eclipse ballroom in Ballyhaunis, County Mayo, I am reminded of a particular gig there. Things were going nicely, with the crowd responding well. I was at the front of the stage, giving my all to a new number, when I saw a rat make his way out from under the stage and casually mooch around the feet of the jiving couples, even pausing at one stage to sit down. The rat did not appear to be at all troubled by the gyrating dancers, but what was even stranger was that the dancers were equally untroubled by the ballroom rodent. Maybe, as they were country people, they were accustomed to seeing them in the fields, or perhaps the rat was a regular! We never found out what he thought of the music.

The Lilac in Enniskeane became the 'in' place and was a real dancing Mecca for West Cork. It had a terrific atmosphere and it drew punters from all over the county. The whole of West Cork was dance-mad and Bandon, Bantry, Dunmanway or Skibbereen might have been okay for a normal dance, but for the birthday, special occasion or big dance night like St Stephen's night, all roads led to Enniskeane. It was like a magnet and, of course, it also provided the cream of the showbands. It was, by the way, painted lilac!

Many of the ballrooms built at the

He never put a foot wrong – Dickie Rock and the Miami showband.

time were huge, barn-like structures, with a fancy, high frontage behind which was a fairly basic, hangar-like building. They were aptly nicknamed 'the breeze-block basilicas', as much for their size as for the huge crowds which any cathedral or basilica of the time would have been pushed to accommodate. Inside they were often cold and barren, with a wooden platform for a stage, and no curtains. A few coloured bulbs were a token gesture to luxury, if they worked, and as for ambience – forget it!

Into this arena came the showband, with the task of captivating and transforming people's lives, if only for one evening. The punter had waited all week for this and was now judge and jury. To the showbands' credit they usually succeeded handsomely.

The spin-off was enormous and widespread. Staff were required to run the new halls, cleaners to clean them. Fleets of coaches were hired to ferry the punters to the ballrooms. Petrol stations prospered. Local pubs did great business. As the showbands became part of the very fabric of young people's lives they affected the fortunes of many others and did a huge amount, not just for the morale of the country, but also for the economy.

There is at least one place in Ireland today where you could still relive the memories of your ballroom days on a permanent basis. The true showband aficionado in search of the perfect 'des res' need look no further than the former Top Hat ballroom site in Dún Laoghaire, County Dublin, which has now been converted into luxury apartments. A penthouse would probably cost you a pretty penny, but it would allow you to reminisce to your heart's content in the knowledge that your living space had once echoed to the finest showband sounds in the land.

Another in the Reynolds's chain: Roseland, Moate.

8. Stars in Waiting:
The Great Performers

*'In the midst of all this I ask myself, is there life
after the Joe Dolan Band?'*
Joe Dolan

B y now, the showband on stage was generally a seven- or eight-piece
group, visually pleasing, smartly dressed, clean-cut, proficient and
keen to play, moving and stepping in unison, rehearsed. The overall
impression was one of competence, professionalism and enjoyment. There

**Masters of the
mike: Brendan
Bowyer (left)
and Dickie
Rock (right).**

BRENDAN BOWYER
THE ROYAL SHOWBAND
WATERFORD

was a zest and an almost missionary zeal about them, as they seemed to revel in the excitement of a new musical world in the making.

I remember vividly when a dance was in full swing, particularly in a jiving set, someone on stage would shout 'across the board' and all the singers along the front of the band would take over from each other, singing a different song one after the other without any break in the medley, thus keeping the dancers on the floor. As we couldn't always hear above the noise, we developed a signalling system to denote the musical key we required. For example, one finger

BRENDAN O'BRIEN

pointed down meant one flat, and the band knew instantly that you wanted the key of F for your song. One finger held up meant one sharp (G), two fingers held down meant B-flat, and so on. As you moved to the mike you made your signal and the band changed to the right key. It was simple but effective. There was no pre-arranged order to the songs but we did know each other's repertoire and, as long as the tempo was the same, we could go on for half an hour, non-stop. A fast session like this was always followed by a very slow set for the best effect, and to allow the dancers to get their breath back.

Although they did not know it, 'stars' were waiting to be discovered and 'frontmen' were destined to become household names. In the beginning, the members of a showband all had more or less equal status, but soon the spotlight began to fall more and more on the vocalists. It was not uncommon for a

Above: Brendan O'Brien of the Dixies. His 'Little Arrows' hit many hearts.
Left: Butch Moore's 'Walking the Streets in the Rain', Ireland's Eurovision entry in 1965, was one of his many hits.

band to have four singers (the Saints had six), each specialising in a particular style – from Jim Reeves numbers to Irish ballads, from rock 'n' roll to country and western. And, as previously mentioned, the Royal had number one hits with three different vocalists: Tom Dunphy, Brendan Bowyer and Charlie Matthews.

The dancers were shrewd and would quickly spot the spark that was igniting the different bands. The reaction of the girls in particular propelled the key men into the spotlight, as they signalled which ones had become their 'heart-throbs'. (I don't think the term 'sex-symbol' was in common currency in those days, and it certainly wasn't bandied about it the conservative Irish dance halls.) Astute managers, always on the lookout for a gimmick, soon cottoned on to what, and who, was really selling a band and the 'star' was born. The Drifters now became Joe Dolan and the Drifters, the Capitol changed to Butch Moore and the Capitol, the Miami became Dickie Rock and the Miami. There was Doc Carroll and the Royal Blues and, of course, Brendan Bowyer was always mentioned in the same breath as the Royal. It was good business practice, as those frontmen had become magnets in their own right and, as

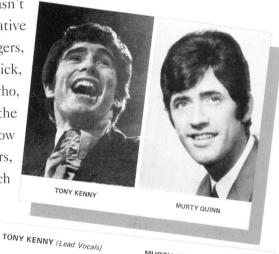

TONY KENNY

MURTY QUINN

TONY KENNY (Lead Vocals)

BIRTHDAY : 14th April
COLOUR OF EYES : Brown
COLOUR OF HAIR : Brown
EDUCATED : Plas Mhuire, Dublin
GROUP OTHER THAN PRESENT ONE : Vampires
FIRST RECORD : "Help Me Rhonda"
RADIO DEBUT : 17 Club
T.V. DEBUT : Late Late Show
BROTHERS/SISTERS : 1 Sister
AMBITIONS : To be as successful as I can for as long as I
CAR : Austin 1100
LIKES : Music, Clothes, Girls
FAVOURITE FOOD : Steak, Ham
FAVOURITE DRINK : Cola
FAVOURITE PLACE : Dublin
FAVOURITE SINGERS (International) : Jack Jones
FAVOURITE GROUPS (International) : The Beatles
FAVOURITE ACTOR : Paul Newman
FAVOURITE SONG : "My Lagan Love"
HOBBIES : Swimming, Walking
JOB BEFORE ENTERING SHOWBUSINESS : Butcher

MURTY QUINN (Trombone)

BIRTHDAY : 5th February
COLOUR OF EYES : Brown
COLOUR OF HAIR : Black
EDUCATED : C.B.S. Dun Laoire
JOB BEFORE ENTERING SHOWBUSINESS : Office Clerk
FIRST RECORD : "There Goes My Everything" and
                    "One Kiss For Old Time's Sake"
RADIO DEBUT : 17 Club
T.V. DEBUT : Showband Show
BROTHERS/SISTERS : 5 Sisters, 2 Brothers
GREATEST MOMENT : Appearing at London Palladium
CAR : Opel Fast Back
LIKES : Sun Bathing
DISLIKES : Getting out of bed
FAVOURITE FOOD : Steak, Melon
FAVOURITE DRINK : Water
FAVOURITE PLACES : Spain, Ireland, Italy
FAVOURITE TYPES OF GIRLS : Girls with a sense of humour
FAVOURITE SINGER : Sammy Davis Jr.
FAVOURITE GROUPS OR BANDS : Bee Gees, Beatles
FAVOURITE ACTORS : Anthony Quinn, Peter O'Toole
FAVOURITE RECORDS : Anything by the Everly Brothers
                        or Sandpipers
HOBBIES : Keeping Fit, Sun-bathing
LUCKY NUMBER : 5
FAVOURITE COLOURS : Red, Blue, Tangerine
FAVOURITE TYPE OF CLOTHING : Casual

**The fans wanted all the details
on Tony Kenny and Murty Quinn of the Sands showband.**

long as they were pulling the punters into the ballrooms, the other band members would not be too resentful. It was a win–win situation.

There was always the danger, however, that the tail might wag the dog – if the star left, the band was in big trouble, as happened when Brendan Bowyer left the Royal to form the Big 8. I always felt that in a showband set-up, the star needed the band's backing as much as they needed him. Where would Big Tom be without the Mainliners, or Larry Cunningham without the Mighty Avons?

Just as the Irish have that gift of being able to tell a tall tale, it was the 'gimp', as it was known, that sold the show – a projection, a knack of delivery that seemed unique to the Irish, that undefined ability to sell the song, to 'smile' through it – and the enjoyment really did seem to radiate from the bandstand. Having seven or eight members in a band was a great advantage, as it enabled individuals to leave the stage to change, or a brass section to leave and re-enter behind the crowd, much to their surprise and delight. It has been estimated that up to seventy percent of showband musicians did not read music, but most were excellent 'luggers' (they could play by ear) and it is my personal belief that far from hindering them, in a strange way it helped and allowed them to perform as naturally as they did. They listened again and again to the record or song they were going to cover, and produced live on stage an exact clone of the number in question. It was as good as, and often better than, the original. They did not have the restriction of being 'glued' to a music part and could move and step freely. Their natural ability shone through all the more for it and sold the number and their show. The diversity of programme, colour and variety helped to keep the whole show fresh and interesting (where the chart groups tended to specialise in one musical style). The music spoke for itself to be sure, but there was a depth to it that belied the effortless simplicity that first impressed the ear.

For the ten years or so, 1957–67, that the showbands were at the height of their creative power, they all appeared to share one quality, apart from their superb stage skills – the ability to keep the punter happy. The hallmark of the top bands was a polished, distinctive and consistent sound, which was unfailingly reproduced night after night after night, sometimes for years. The reputation of the showband 'charm school' is legendary, with many of the artists bringing their own particular style to their craft. Who will forget seeing Fergie O'Hagan (Clipper Carlton), sporting a Stetson, saunter casually forward to sit on the edge of stage, push his Stetson nonchalantly back on his head and with the crowd around him do his monologue, 'Life gets tedious'. Where other singers would have just come to the microphone to do the number 'straight', O'Hagan's performance really sold the piece and it became a memorable and essential part of the band's repertoire. I can recall another singer who at the start of his special number clicked his fingers and the lights instantly went out. Dickie Rock would swing his microphone on stage, Sonny Knowles acquired the nickname 'The Window Cleaner' for his habit of waving his hand in a circle, palm out, while performing special numbers. It was show business with a capital 'S'. Other notable showmen in this sense were Brendan Bowyer, Joe McCarthy, Butch Moore, Joe Dolan and Larry Cunningham, and any dancer from that era would immediately be able to tell you what each of their special trademarks were.

Opposite: Doc Carroll of the Royal Blues. The band had a big hit with 'Old Man Trouble'. Doc is still regularly entertaining on the cabaret circuit. Right: the man from 'Lovely Leitrim', Larry Cunningham.

9. From Waltz to Hucklebuck: The Dancers

'There have been so many fringe benefits, like world travel, meeting with people of different nationalities and cultures, valued and cherished friendships, and so many wonderful memories in the process. I suppose the opportunity of getting together with movie stars, rock stars, top politicians and sports stars has been rather special, but as often happens, the seemingly unimportant on the world stage prove to be the most special of all. I've been truly blessed.'

Brendan Bowyer

Dancers all over Ireland had a major role to play in the showband saga. Without them there would have been no stars, no ballrooms, no showband business. They were your audience, your customers, your critics and your judges. You ignored their wants at your peril, and while Irish audiences were always willing to 'give a listen' to something new, you very quickly gauged from their reaction whether it was something to keep in the act or drop. They had paid good money for four or five hours of entertainment, for escape from their daily lives and, hopefully, for a spot of romance 'after the ball was over'. And most showbands realised that the key to success was to attract a following of girls – where the girls went, the lads would follow, believe me! They were as astute as they were charming and they knew what they wanted from a band. If you provided it, you got the crowds. As Larry Cunningham put it, 'You never saw the floorboards.' You instinctively knew when you had got the formula right, as you could feel the rapport with the crowd coming back at you on stage.

The Royal Showband giving it their all at the Crystal ballroom.

And could they dance? Yes, they could. It seemed to me that everybody in Ireland danced, and most of them danced very well, although I'm sure there are some ladies out there whose scarred feet would say otherwise. I remember learning to dance that great standby, 'The Old-Time Waltz', at the Technical College dances in Rathmines Town Hall. If you were to have any luck in the 'ladies stakes', you had to try to give yourself an edge and some smooth moves on the dance floor did you no harm at all. Later, when I was providing the music, I was always impressed at the speed with which a new dance would take on. A fortnight after the release of Brendan Bowyer's 'Hucklebuck', we played in a hall in Achill and the dancers had every step off to perfection: 'Wiggle like a snake, waddle like a duck, that's what you do when you do the Hucklebuck.' It was the same in whatever county you performed – the dancers wanted to hear it and you were in big trouble if you didn't play it.

And don't we laugh now when we look back at the photos, in the same way that our kids laugh at pictures of their parents when they were teens – their turn will come! But I thought the effort the dancers put into the way they looked then was smashing. The girls looked stunning in their simple A-line dresses and beehive hairdos. The lads were always attired in the requisite two-piece suit and sporting any colour shirt you could wish for as long as it was

Brendan Bowyer shows 'the Hucklebuck Girls' how it's done.

white. Life was so much less complicated back in those days. The pointed 'winkle-picker' shoes were highly polished and the ties neatly knotted, the more fashionable favouring the Windsor knot. When the slow sets were played, a heady mixture of Brylcreem and hair lacquer wafted up towards the stage. There were dress standards then – and they were upheld. It was not uncommon for dancers to travel up to sixty miles to hear their favourite band and these people then danced until 2am before the return journey home and Monday morning's work.

The Sunday night dance became the highlight of the week and was discussed for several days afterwards. But any youngsters (ie. under fifty) who are reading this might ask: Why Sunday? Why not Saturday? Well, it was down to the influence wielded by the clergy at that time. In those days, there were no afternoon Masses on Sundays and the Saturday evening vigil Mass was unheard of, so the only choice for the devout population was the Sunday morning Mass, the last one usually beginning at twelve noon. Maybe the thinking of the priests was that any of their flock who had spent Saturday night dancing till all hours, possibly drinking and, God forbid, maybe up to some debauchery, would be unable, unwilling or unfit to appear in the house of the Lord or Sunday morning. Whatever the reasoning behind it, Saturday night dancing was banned or severely restricted in most parts of the country. Saturday night, as they say in Las Vegas, was 'dark'.

From the stage we had a great view of everything that was happening on the dance floor, and as I gazed down through the blue haze of cigarette smoke, I was often hugely entertained by the events unfolding in front of me: the engaged couple having a tiff because some other lad had asked her to dance, or a visiting girl down from Dublin being chased by three different lads. Tradi-

Right: 'You never saw the floorboards'

tionally there was always one dance a night that was 'ladies choice', when the girls could ask the male of their fancy to dance with them. This was very interesting to watch from the bandstand as the chosen lad tried to act matter-of-fact and casual, while the other suitors threw in the towel. It was not unusual to see men of seventy dancing with girls of eighteen and I have it on good authority that they could be much more of a handful and harder to handle than any nineteen year old: 'You could control the youngsters because you knew their sisters.'

It was still common in a lot of the ballrooms for the males to line up on one side and the females on the other. The tentative, hesitant progress of the lads across that vast expanse of floor to ask the fancied girl for a dance was sometimes painful to watch. Granted, their technique was sadly lacking in finesse – often just a jerk of the head, or the oft-quoted, 'Are ye dancing?' to which the standard reply was, 'Are ye asking?' You always hoped that they would not be turned down. That long 'walk of shame' back to the ranks must have been awful. I suppose it must have been equally shattering for the girl who wasn't asked up at all and ended up being a 'wallflower' for the entire night. I gather, however, that the ladies had some strategies of their own to attract a partner, and I know of one who would divert a lad on his way to ask someone else to dance with the remark, 'Lovely hair – did you knit it yourself?' Surprisingly, it usually worked.

Overseas acts and bands visiting Ireland's ballrooms are universal in their acclaim of the Irish dancing public and have all been impressed by their warm and enthusiastic reception, the energy and friendliness of the crowds during the performance and the sincere appreciation at its conclusion. The showbands themselves will surely agree that they were swept along by the same re-ception and lifted to new heights of endeavour and performance. One of the lovely things about it was that the bands in any corner or county in Ireland were always made to feel at home and welcome. They have a lot to thank those punters for.

'Put your hands in the air'. The Miami showband perform 'Simple Simon Says' at the Arcadia ballroom, Bray, 1968.

10. The Northern Showbands: Pathfinders

'There was a time in this town when a man couldn't throw a stone at random and fail to hit a past, present or soon-to-be member of a showband.'
Gerry Anderson, TV and Radio presenter, Derry

The Monarchs from Belfast, featuring a young Van Morrison (seated, second left) and George Jones (seated, right).

The musical talent did not stop at the border and showbands from Northern Ireland were not going to be outdone by their cousins in the South. In fact, as already mentioned, they initially led the way in the form of 'the daddy of them all', the Clipper Carlton from Strabane. They set the standard and established the showband tradition of hard work and musical expertise allied to showmanship and professionalism.

If the Clipper Carlton were the first, a close second had to be the Melody Aces, a

band from Newtownstewart, County Tyrone, who were spoiled for top vocalists in the persons of Shay Hutchinson, David Coyle and Gene Turbett. From their first big break in Galway back in the 'fifties, they became hugely popular, with a loyal and ardent follow- ing all over Ireland. Gene Turbett recalled to me that

THE VENTURES SHOWBAND
FAN CLUB SECRETARY: HELEN CULLAINE C/O LIAM DONNELLY
Monaghan Rd. Aughnacloy, Co. Fermanagh. Phone Aughnacloy 283.

they were paid £25 for that Galway gig; it was the furthest they had been from home and they stayed overnight, making them feel really professional. While the Aces did not include a cabaret spot like the Clipper Carlton's in their programme, they nevertheless kept the dancers happy with a bright, cheerful style of presentation that seemed to go down particularly well in rural areas. Their success was further boosted when they were selected as the band to open the first of the Reynolds brothers' chain of rural ballrooms, the Cloudland at Rooskey. Shay Hutchinson, who had a fine singing voice, is widely acknowledged as the man who popularised and introduced country and western into the showband world. He has been quoted as saying, 'I came to stand in with the band for one night and stayed for twenty years.' I am happy to report that as I write this, in year two of a new millennium, Shay Hutchinson is still singing. Strangely, considering how popular they were, the Melody Aces remain today some- what unsung in the annals of showband history, but for me they will always be one of the central pillars on which the whole business was built.

PLATTERMEN
with
BRIAN COLL

First Record "KATHLEEN"

Coupling with "I'm in Love Again"
NOW ON SALE

The Johnny Quigley Allstars from Derry were different in style from the Aces, but were without doubt one of the finest all-round showbands it has been my pleasure to hear and enjoy. They successfully made the transition from dance band to showband, and with Roy Adinell playing a fine trumpet, Johnny Peel on lead vocals and Mick Quigley featured on a rasping baritone sax, their take-off of the Coasters was no less than brilliant. Their Dixieland version of 'Onions', vocal harmonies in 'It's a Sin', and their comedy in 'Along came Jones' and 'Run Samson Run' was inspiring stuff – it certainly worked for me. When you see good leadership you follow. I'm not ashamed to say that we were quick to copy any good numbers we heard, and we certainly did a few of Johnny Quigley's. I consider this to be the ultimate accolade to a fellow band.

Omagh produced the Plattermen, who included Rob Strong, still performing today. Rob is also the father of Andrew Strong, of *The Commitments* fame.

Whatever its secret, Derry had an uncanny knack of turning out top-class bands – in addition to the Allstars, it also produced the Barristers, the Jokers, the Embassy, the Esquires, the Emperors, the Kingston and the International, to name but a few. Another visitor from over the border who was always welcome was Dave Glover – a superb band musically. Muriel Day, who sang with the band, became Dave's wife and peformed 'Wages of Love', Ireland's entry in the 1969 Eurovision Song Contest. I was lucky enough to catch him twenty-five years later when he played Coventry's Hippodrome Theatre, and yes, the magic was still there. The Witnesses would also have to be included in that exclusive club of great Northern bands, as anyone who heard them would readily testify.

The North provided what was recognised nationally as Ireland's finest vocal harmony group, the Freshmen from Ballymena, County Antrim, a very modern band musically by showband standards. Fronted and influenced by Billy Brown and Derek Dean, their 'Beach Boys' sound, their multiple harmonies and their presentation was considered so good that they were invited to play on the same bill as their Californian counterparts when the Beach Boys appeared in Belfast. The general consensus was that the Irish boys were the more polished act musically, vocally and visually, and no less a personage than the late Rory Gallagher, who was present at the show, has been quoted as confirming this fact. The Freshmen were also very shrewd operators and, while their vocal abilities were unquestionable, they also realised the importance of good sound equipment, and spent liberally on it. It is probably safe to say that they had more showstoppers than any other band in the business, and whenever they performed the old Tremeloes classic, silence really was 'golden' as their audiences stood spellbound.

**Top: Derek Deane.
Right: Derek, Billy Brown and the
Freshmen – better harmonies
than the Beach Boys.**

11. That Binson Echo: Making the Showband Sound

'It was a real pleasure to be part of the showband revolution, and a privilege to be associated with all those people involved in it.'

Paddy Cole, the Capitol showband

In the beginning, the PA system in common use was unbelievably basic. The early bands, knowing no different, happily played through an 80w amp and two 2 x 12' speaker cabinets. The old Vortexion valve amplifier was then much in evidence and you had to wind the two bare speaker wires onto two lugs at the back and secure them by tightening the nuts – honest! On more than one occasion I have seen mains power supply leads, with no plug, have their bare ends inserted into live sockets and held in place by matchsticks. Shocking stuff, in more senses than one. The power supply in the early marquees defied logic, reason and belief, not to mention safety regulations, but it always seemed to work. It passed for modern technology in those days.

Art O'Hagan, bass player with the Clipper Carlton, also controlled the band's sound system and he reminded me recently of the problem we all had when trying to project the sound down the five-pole marquees of the time. Art would walk the length of the floor as the boys played a number with the

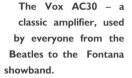

The Vox AC30 – a
classic amplifier, used
by everyone from the
Beatles to the Fontana
showband.

amplifier on maximum
volume. He recalls:
'There would be 2,500
dancers in the marquee,
and by the time I had
reached the second pole I
couldn't hear a thing from the
stage, but they were all dancing away,
oblivious.'

The story is told of an occasion when Tommy Drennan
and the Monarchs, from Limerick, were playing in a marquee
when the electricity finally gave up the ghost. The venue was
plunged into total darkness – no sound equipment, no lights, nothing. Un-
daunted, the carnival committee brought a motor car into the centre of the
marquee, switched the headlights on to full beam, and the band belted away
with only an accordion and drums for musical accompaniment. After every set
the whole seven band members had to shout in unison, 'Your next dance,
please.' A very practical and Irish solution, but the show went on. The inci-
dent says a lot for the temperament and easy-going nature of the dancers back
then; there would be uproar today.

The erratic power supply, the low-tech amplification and the small parish
halls, which were the usual venues prior to the construction of the big ballroom chains, were far from ideal conditions in which to put on good entertainment. There was a lot of enthusiasm, but the sound was poor and very sadly
lacking in quality and clarity. Fortunately, the dancers did not mind or even
notice; they were conditioned to it. But the showbands drove for change re-
lentlessly, as the musicians cried out for more, and better, equipment. And it
came in the form of two Marmac 'Crazy Box' speaker cabinets, containing ten
speakers per 'cab'. These were designed by Dermot Hurley in Dublin and

were the showbands' first experience of 100-volt line. We didn't understand how it worked then, and still don't understand it today, but the sound was colossal and really surpassed itself in the marquees of the time. I remember the speaker cabinets having a piece of rope protruding through the top panel, the idea being that you would hang the speaker on convenient hooks, which, of course, were never there. Some bands resorted to carrying their own 'S' hooks, which solved the problem on most occasions. If you were very lucky, very successful or both, these speaker cabs were powered by a 'Dynacord' 200-watt Gigant power amp. To his credit, Glenamaddy's Joe O'Neill was well ahead of the rest in providing this equipment and as the more successful bands beat a constant track to his door, he did very nicely, thank you.

The bullhead Shure microphone.

The new equipment proved a vast improvement and a great success. It became the benchmark, the ideal, and finally the standard. When we eventually acquired one, I can clearly remember the great difference it made to our sound reproduction. I almost believed I could sing! It was every young band's dream to get such a 'rig'.

You could always spot the showband musicians at a dance, because they showed great interest in scrutinising the sound system, while the average dancer couldn't care where the sound came from as long as it was good. The old bullhead Shure 'mike' – robust, practical, reliable, multi-directional – was ideal for brass and built for the rigours of the road, so was still much in evidence. But it gradually made way for the 'pencil' unidyne Shure, which, because it perfectly suited the slick visual image that the showband frontmen were trying to project, became the chosen microphone of most vocalists.

Some of the improvements were a mixed blessing. In the Saints we were fortunate to have a full-sized Hammond organ with a Leslie speaker. It had a superb sound, but we often queried its worth after struggling to carry it up five flights of stairs. The problem was half solved when we acquired an army stretcher and, by bolting the arms to the sides of the Hammond, we were able

Above: 'You could hear that Binson echo round the marquee in Drumlish.'

to lift it more easily.

Most bands favoured a Farfisa or Vox Continental, which were much smaller and more portable organs, and I can well understand why, as there were no 'roadies' back then to do the lifting and carrying.

The next major milestone was the introduction of the 'Binson' – a portable echo chamber. It would have set you back about £165, a lot of money in 1962. When first introduced by the Royal showband and heard at a live gig, it was a revelation in vocal reproduction. The young and vibrant business sat up and took notice and it became the goal of every aspiring band to acquire one. What a difference it made to the previously dry sound! Suddenly vocals were enhanced, full, rich and resonant. The advert for the Binson had screamed, 'The definitive and most successful electro-mechanical echo unit ever built,' and it lived up to its billing. I recall first using one – the Binson Echorec 2 model – in the Town Hall in Mullingar on an Easter Sunday night and being totally captivated. Although there was a natural tendency to overdo the echo initially, when mastered and adjusted correctly it became a vital and integral part of every showband's equipment. All veteran showband punters knew exactly what he meant when, forty years later, Declan Nerney was to sing, 'You could hear that Binson echo round the marquee in Drumlish.'

The Binson was such a success that most lead guitarists began to use an additional unit solely to further enhance the sound of their favoured guitar, the Fender 'Strat'. The Fender Stratocaster guitar was then retailing at about £160. One particular 'Strat' has a well-chronicled history: Jim Conlon of the Royal showband had wanted a red Fender Strat, like the one played by Hank Marvin of the Shadows, but the guitar he got was in a finish known as 'sunburst'. He traded it in part-exchange for a new red one from Crowley's music shop, Cork. The sunburst guitar was put back on display. A young musician came in and bought it for £100. The musician was Rory Gallagher and that 1961 Fender Stratocaster became his trademark as it accompanied him, battered and scratched but still capable of producing his unique sound, until the untimely end of his brilliant career in 1995. It lay on the hearse at his funeral in Cork.

In terms of equipment and technology, the showbands had come a long way from the days when a car battery was often used to drive the PA equipment and a hefty push was required to start the car for the journey home.

A 'sunburst' Fender Stratocaster – the instrument of choice for the great **Rory Gallagher**.

12. The Dublin Scene: The Crystal, Ierne and National

'Had anyone told me in 1962 that people would still be talking about the showband era in 2002, I would not have believed them.'

Eileen Reed, the Cadets showband

No book on the showband era would be complete without reference to the dancing scene in the Dublin of the early 1960s. It was diverse, dynamic and booming – a 'happening' place, just as it is today. So many people from the rest of Ireland worked, studied in, or visited Dublin regularly that the dancehalls of the capital were known far and wide. The names trip off the tongue like a familiar roll-call: the Ierne, the National, the Town and Country, all located around Parnell Square; Clery's and the Metropole on O'Connell Street; the Four Provinces (later renamed the Television Club) in Harcourt Street; the Crystal; the Olympic; and Barry's Hotel, to name just a few.

If my memory is right, there were dances in Dublin seven nights a week. O'Connell Street would be thronged just after two o'clock each morning, as the dances finished and the crowds poured out to head for home. Each ballroom had its own particular atmosphere and catered for a dedicated clientele, so the bands were selected with great care to maintain this. The National was

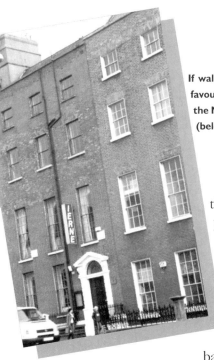

If walls could speak! Three of Dublin's favourite dance halls: the Ierne (left), the National (right) and Barry's Hotel (below).

the chosen venue for lots of visitors 'up from the country' and for many of the large number of provincial workers who made their living in the capital city, so the bands who played there had to cater for that audience. The venue was affectionately known as 'the Corncrushers', for fairly obvious reasons. It always attracted a host of the country girls who were staying in hostels in Henrietta Street or Mountjoy Square before making the big move out to their first bedsit, because you could just make the weekend late curfew by running all the way home from Parnell Square, whereas this would not have been possible from dance halls further afield. The programme in the National would have contained a fair share of country and western, a lot of old-time waltzes and a lot of up-tempo music for which jiving was the order of the day. The clientele felt comfortable with this, as it was what they would hear back in their home towns.

In contrast, the Television Club (formerly the Four Provinces) on Harcourt Street would be packing in the native Dubliners, who favoured a more modern and up-to-date programme. Country and western music and old-time waltzes would have little appeal to this crowd. I always got a great kick out of playing there. The crowd was very well up – they knew all the songs, and there was great 'craic' and banter from the stage with the girls on the balcony. On Monday nights the venue became the established meeting place for the showbands on their night off. New contacts were discussed, telephone numbers acquired, opinions on the merits of new band equipment exchanged. If you needed to see someone in the showband business, it was the place to look. Strangely enough, apart from at the Television Club or just passing them on the road, you did not see very much of other bands, and rarely got the chance to watch them in action. Everybody was always playing gigs at different ends of the country, so the Monday night get-together became a fixture.

CAPITOL SHOWBAND

I also enjoyed playing the Ierne, another great Mecca of the Dublin dancing scene, where Christy Gunn welcomed both the bands and the dancers alike. Every showband of any significance played there, and it was always packed. It also has another claim to fame: it was where Dickie Rock met his wife, Judy. The Ierne was the very last 'dry' ballroom in the city, never selling alcohol and providing only tea, coffee or minerals. However, it has to be said that these seemed to provide enough of a 'kick' to keep the dancers going all night. It closed its doors for the last time in June 2000, and many showband veterans and dancers marked its passing with regret.

The Town and Country was more irreverently known to regulars as 'the Town and Bog'. It was not uncommon for girls who had suffered the rigours of a weekend at Lough Derg to head straight into the dance hall in Dublin on their way back, still existing on the cups of black tea and burnt toast served on the retreat. Now there's commitment for you!

Brendan Bowyer. His powerful voice and energetic on-stage performances made the man from Waterford the most popular vocalist of the entire showband era. He had numerous No 1 hits with The Royal showband. Now based in Las Vegas, he is still a regular performer.

BEST WISHES
for
CHRISTMAS
and
THE NEW YEAR
from
BIG TOM & THE MAINLINERS

MAPLE BALLROOM,
ROCKCORRY.

Christmas Greetings from Big Tom McBride. Fans were hungry for any kind of showband souvenir. Cards and autographed publicity shots became treasured possessions.

Tom Jones and Brendan O'Brien at The Point, Dublin.

Left: Colour, style and that famous hair-do. The Cadets made a big impact.

Right: The Freshmen, led by Derek Deane and Billy Brown, were regarded as one of the most creative and original bands around.

Below: The Capitol were regular chart-toppers. In 1964 **Spotlight** readers voted them Ireland's No 2 showband. They had a wealth of talent, including Butch Moore, Don Long and Paddy Cole.

THE FRESHMEN

Right: The Drifters. 'The Answer to Everything' was the first of numerous hit records. Joe Dolan's unique voice and stage presence continue to make him a hugely popular performer.

Left: The Victors showband from Cork, led by Art Supple.

The Victors

Right: 'Old Man Trouble' himself, Doc Carroll.

Above: Dickie Rock and The Miami had a string of hits, including 'There's Always Me', 'From the Candy Store on the Corner', and 'Every Step of the Way'. Now performing cabaret, Dickie is one of Ireland's most successful entertainers.

Right: About as far from the dance band image of black suits and dickie bows as one could get. The Gaylords are in the pink!

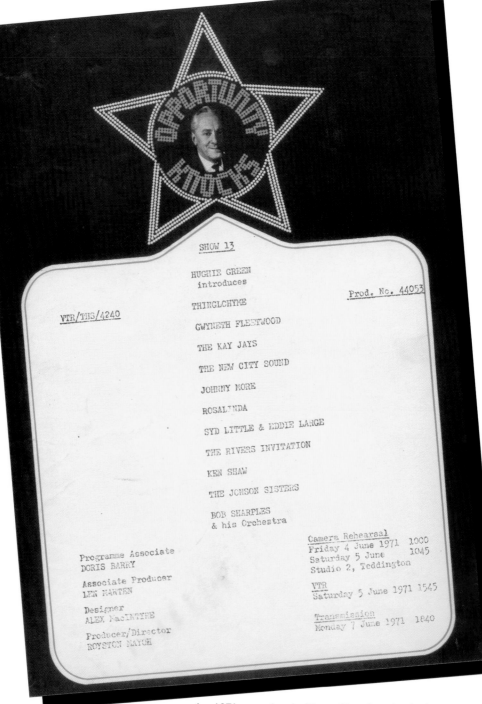

SHOW 13

HUGHIE GREEN
introduces

Prod. No. 44053

VTR/THS/4240

THINGLCHYME

GWYNETH FLEETWOOD

THE KAY JAYS

THE NEW CITY SOUND

JOHNNY MORE

ROSALINDA

SYD LITTLE & EDDIE LARGE

THE RIVERS INVITATION

KEN SHAW

THE JOHSON SISTERS

BOB SHARPLES
& his Orchestra

Programme Associate
DORIS BARRY

Associate Producer
LEN MARTEN

Designer
ALEX MacINTYRE

Producer/Director
ROYSTON MAYOH

Camera Rehearsal
Friday 4 June 1971   1000
Saturday 5 June   1045
Studio 2, Teddington

VTR
Saturday 5 June 1971 1545

Transmission
Monday 7 June 1971 1840

In 1971, my band, New City Sounds, had a three-week run on Hughie Green's famous TV talent show: 'Opportunity Knocks'.

Three very different styles of showband:
The Sands with Tony Kenny (above, left),
Sean Fagan and the Pacific (right);
below: The Premier Aces.

PREMIER ACES SHOWBAND   BALLINTUBBER, CO. ROSCOMMON   Phone 10

Chart Topping

REAL McCOY

FAN CLUB: PATRICIA GRENNAN,
50 LOWER BEECHWOOD AVENUE,
RANELAGH, DUBLIN 6.

Above: The Real McCoy having fun at Portmarnock Beach, Dublin. The band had a No 1 hit with 'Quick Joey Small.'

Left: Athlone's 'The Showband Show', fronted by Loraine and Keith McDonald, successfully replicate the sound and style of the 'sixties showbands and back the major stars of the period on regular nationwide tours.

Bands based in Dublin had a distinct advantage in that they were at the hub of the wheel, with any number of dance halls and ballrooms within easy reach. It was perhaps the heartbeat of the whole showband industry, and definitely the place to be. Whatever was happening happened in Dublin first. The bands had ready access to the large musical equipment stores, to national newspapers for advertising, to printing and publicity houses, to stagewear shops and even to coachbuilders for their bandwagons. Another big plus was that the national television station was on their doorstep. Of course, the Dublin bands took full advantage.

The music makers of the first city became household names and carried the showband banner proudly and high. They were known and acknowledged nationwide. Bands like the Miami, the Cadets, the Capitol and the Pacific set a standard for style, musical ability and presentation. The Miami were slick, smart, rehearsed and polished. The Cadets were showy but solid, distinctive in their bright, naval-style uniforms. They were fronted by vocalist Eileen Reed, famous for her elaborate hairstyle and her 'My Wedding Dress' song, for which she wore a real wedding outfit. The Capitol were professional and balanced and made it all look so easy – the true mark of the experts. The Pacific always gave a solid, reliable backing to the vocal talents of Sonny Knowles and Sean Fagan. What strikes me as I write this, so many years later, is just how many of the names from these bands are still entertaining people today, among them Eileen Reed, Dickie Rock and Sonny Knowles. That is some achievement.

In the same way that different bands suited different venues and

The Pacific: another big-name band, with Sean Fagan (centre, front) and the evergreen Sonny Knowles (standing, left).

audiences, it would be fair also to say that some Dublin bands did not quite 'crack it' in the more rural country ballrooms, where their polished, slick style and their programmes were perhaps considered too sophisticated. It was 'horses for courses', and is more of a comment on the tastes of punters than on the abilities of particular bands. There is no question that the shows many Dublin bands put on were done extremely well and in their field they were unsurpassable. The showband annals today clearly reflect this. I can recall the Miami playing the Emerald ballroom, Ballinasloe, in the early 1960s, when I happened to sneak in a small tape recorder as they rehearsed before the gig. I sat quietly in the balcony and recorded 'The Hawaiian Wedding Song' (an Elvis number from the film *Blue Hawaii*) as they polished up the harmonies; they must have run through the number at least seven times. Realising what I was doing, they came up to the balcony and then listened to and analysed the song a further six or seven times. Dedication, dedication, dedication! I so wish I had that recording today.

NOW ON SALE
MY WEDDING DRESS
CHAPEL OF LOVE

Eileen Reed in full bridal regalia for her smash
hit tearjerker 'My Wedding Dress'.

13. Coosan Schoolhouse Rock: The Rehearsal

The old 'sitting-down' bands had a set programme of familiar tunes, most of which remained popular for years. The showbands, on the other hand, because they covered so many of of the current chart-toppers, had to keep changing their programmes to keep up with the latest hits. Regular rehearsals were vital. The trick was to try to gauge the new releases that were going to make a real impact, rehearsing those numbers as they began their climb up the pop charts, and therefore get the most mileage possible from the number. There was not a lot of point doing a number after it had peaked and was on the slide. In short, 'must do' numbers were agreed and selected as they 'began to bubble', judged on airplay regularity, chart entry or the popularity of the recording artiste. The band member with the most suitable singing style would be picked to cover the number on stage. He would be expected to tape the song from the radio on that week's 'Top Twenty Show' or from Radio Luxembourg, listen to it and memorise it for the following week's rehearsal. There was always intense competition to sing the really big hits – tact and diplomacy were often called for and egos had to be skilfully massaged. Common sense generally prevailed in the long run and, like most

'Where the Shannon waters flow'. The Saints take a moment out from rehearsing.

bands, the Saints had an accepted Jim Reeves, Tom Jones, Engelbert Humperdink or Johnny Cash singer to handle their respective numbers. Brass men would meanwhile listen for any brass figures or riffs, while the rhythm section would be checking out the rhythm and chord sequences.

We were fortunate that Syd Shine, our bandleader, had bought the old Coosan National School, just outside Athlone, for the princely sum of £900. All our rehearsals were held there. They were simple but effectively-structured affairs, typically commencing at about 1pm. A suitable key for a song would be decided upon first, always to accommodate the singer's vocal range. The brass section would then work on their riffs and harmonies at one end of the room, while the singer and rhythm section listened to and polished up the intro and chord sequence. When both parties were reasonably happy, they would combine and collectively 'go for it'. A relatively straightforward number generally took thirty or forty minutes to sound reasonable. From the first tentative chords it began to finally come together with the addition of the rhythm section and full-blown brass. There was great satisfaction when things worked out particularly well and the number began to actually resemble the original record. We would then decide on the steps and movements to accompany the music. After four or five runs, we would move on to the next song. There was the occasional heated moment, such as an argument about what chord was right or how something should be done, but generally the problem was discussed sensibly and a compromise reached without bloodshed.

This format seemed to work well for us, principally because we all came to rehearsal fairly well prepared. We had a great advantage in that the four of us who had been in the army band still spent our leisure time together every day, so the songs and ideas had already been well kicked around before we ever turned up for rehearsal. Consequently, our brass section was very strong. We sometimes performed brass arrangements of numbers like 'The William Tell Overture' or 'The Dambusters', which added great colour to the programme. The punter was not to know that we had played these every day anyway in our 'real' army jobs, and of course we never told them.

In the four hours of rehearsal we would generally work out three numbers, but I can remember doing five. The newly rehearsed numbers would then be played two or three times a night for the first week, by which time they became second nature and you could play them in your sleep. And then the work began all over again.

But it was all worth it when you got on stage.

The old Coosan National School, outside Athlone, was the rehearsal hall for the Saints.

14. A Gig at the Pavesi

Lucky girl!

typical night's work – a gig at the Pavesi ballroom, Donegal town, 30 June 1963:

3pm: Frank Somers, drummer with The Saints, is fuelling up our bandwagon, registration number WI 8434, at Gill's Garage, Athlone. The days of the Zephyr 4 are long gone – this bus, which we bought from Waterford's Blue Aces, is customised and kitted out for comfort with aircraft seats, wardrobes and all mod cons. The wheels are scheduled to roll at 3.30.

3.25pm: All the members of the Saints are gathered at the pickup point – Syd Shine's converted barge on the River Shannon. We finally get going at 3.40. Ireland's roads are not very good at this time, bearing no relation to the motorways of 2002, so it takes a long time to get anywhere. There are no service areas and telephones are few and far between. The journey to Donegal will take approximately three-and-a-half-hours; the time will be spent listening to some new numbers on the tape recorder and having the 'craic'.

The very same scene is being played out at 500 or 600 locations all over Ireland, as the country's showbands set out on their various journeys to fulfil bookings at venues in every one of the thirty-two counties. Already several bandwagons have crossed Athlone Bridge, heading east, west, north and south, always with a cheery wave to those spending a lazy afternoon sitting on the town bridge watching the world go by.

7pm: The journey was free of breakdowns, roadworks and traffic jams (these are pretty rare), so the band are now enjoying some of the best steaks in Ireland, at the Abbey Hotel on the Diamond in Donegal town.

The Pavesi has always been a good gig for us and we are looking forward to it. It is a bright and relatively new ballroom that can hold about 1,800. We are confident of filling it to capacity. Having eaten at the Abbey, we head for the ballroom for the set-up and sound checks.

Roadies are as yet unheard of in the showband game, so we do all our own 'pulling and dragging'. We consider this no bad thing, as it means that expensive equipment is treated with due care. Even the set-up is a professional business. The drums are attended to first, as this ensures that the drummer has plenty of room, especially if the stage area is limited. Next come the backline amps, and anything else needed at the back of the stage. Finally come the frontline mikes. There is an unwritten law that dictates that you do not put a single instrument on stage until all of this is completed, as many an expensive saxophone, guitar or trombone has been toppled and badly damaged by somebody pulling a lead or shifting an amp. If you really want to become unpopular, you unpack and put your instrument on stage while all this is going on.

The Saints with 'adoring fans' after a gig at the Pavesi ballroom, Donegal.

8.10pm: 'Testing, testing, one, two.' With the soundcheck completed, it is time to freshen up and change.

8.30pm: Some of the boys are having the proverbial 'jar' or two.

8.45pm: The usual twenty-five or thirty 'early birds' – mostly girls – arrive and wait expectantly. The male population is (yes, you've guessed it) in the pub.

9pm: Action stations. We begin our programme.

The backbone of any decent showband programme lies in playing sixty percent good solid standards like 'North to Alaska', 'Yesterday Man', 'Ring of Fire', 'Be My Guest' and 'My Wild Irish Rose'. These should be very well rehearsed, as they will not generally change. Twenty-five percent of the remainder of the set is composed of current and up-to-date favourites, which will be gradually dropped and replaced after eight or nine weeks. Then you need your 'showstoppers' – the big production numbers that set your showband apart, that 'stamp' your band. Our regular showstoppers include 'Oh Mein Papa' and 'The Holy City', and comedy routines such as 'Jake the Peg' and 'The Laughing Policeman'. These are the numbers we will be remembered for, because as the term suggests, they will (hopefully) stop the dancing.

Bing there, done that. I continued singing, but ditched the hankie!

The Saints have done their homework. When you rehearse, share and enjoy playing together, the feeling of fellowship in a good band is a powerful

phenomenon – more so than in any other profession. You are totally depend-
ent on the people on stage with you. The mutual feeling of respect is rein-
forced after every gig. As you play, you are confident that a certain chord, run,
solo or cymbal crash will happen exactly when it should happen – right on cue,
every time. Conversely, in a poor band, where the respect and confidence is
missing, there is uncertainty, hesitation, indecision and confusion, which can
end in accusation and even confrontation. If you are feeling uncertain, the
audience will pick up on it in a second.

The programme begins with the newer, recently rehearsed numbers, to
help memorise and polish them before the hall fills up. The words of these
have been written out and are pinned to the back of one of the boys on stage,
who positions himself discreetly and strategically just to the front of the
singer. These songs will be repeated later in the evening. The girls are already
jiving together and the hall is gradually filling. For the first two hours, the
numbers are generally lively and up-tempo. All the stops are pulled out for the
last hour-and-a-half, with slow ballad sets before the end.

I am: The night traditionally ends with a rendition of the national anthem,
'Amhrán na bhFiann' (The Soldiers Song). Performance-wise it is probably
the most important number of the night as it is always given due respect and
silence, with the whole crowd standing. The band are well aware that,
because of that full attention, it will leave a lasting impression – good, or bad –
and it is played with that in mind. While some other bands prefer a slow and
more musical rendition, the Saints version is proud and strident, a moving
march tempo. We like to send the punters home with a spring in their step.

At the end of the evening the instruments are packed away
first, again for safety
reasons. Anyone whose
instrument gets dam-
aged through careless
set-up receives no sym-
pathy. It just should not
have been there. Once

everything has been taken down and packed away we take to the road again.

Frank, our drummer, doesn't drink, so he is the nominated driver. I always feel sorry for him, as he misses out on the camaraderie in the back of the van and the 'post-mortem' on the night's events. After the buzz wears off, a contented tiredness sets in – some of the lads are nodding off by the time we get a few miles down the road. The rest talk about the dance, gauging the success of the new numbers, trying to estimate the size of the crowd, and discussing plans for the rest of the week. Sometimes the homeward journeys are really enjoyable, as we roll along quietly in the darkness on lonely roads deep in the country, with the wind howling and rain lashing the windows. The odd graveyard looms up out of the night, and the stories turn to hauntings and other ghostly happenings. Believe me, in this sort of atmosphere, the tales become very real indeed, and if you aren't lucky enough to have nodded off early, you certainly won't sleep after this. Who would miss it?

5.30am: Luckily, we have avoided any incidents and misfortunes, and are now arriving back in Athlone. Who says bands don't earn their money?

Thursday was always payday. At 3pm we would gather at Syd Shine's boat and he would 'divvy out' the week's takings among the band members, less what was owed to our manager, who was paid the same as a band member, plus his expenses. It was all cash, no cheques or bank drafts, so you ended up with your share   in fivers, pound notes, ten-shilling notes, and yes,

lots of half-crowns and smaller coins. We didn't mind – it was still money, whether it rustled or rattled! I can't say that this ever happened to me, but I have heard of people in the top bands taking out a suit from the wardrobe and finding £80 or more in the pocket, where they would have hung it up after a gig and just forgotten about it.

After an absence of thirty-odd years, while driving through Donegal town, I was amazed at how the Abbey Hotel that I remembered as small, friendly and local had expanded and prospered. I noticed also by the posters that it was now a prime music venue in the town. I succumbed to an irresistible urge to drive out to the Pavesi ballroom, and later wished I hadn't. In place of the ballroom that once throbbed to the exciting sounds of the nation's top showbands, I was saddened to find a graffiti-covered, badly run down, neglected building. Which of us could have envisaged this back in the euphoria of the 'sixties boom days? I reflected on how fickle fate is and how, when change is dictated, there is so little we can do to stand in its path.

15. 'The Showband Show': A Showcase to the Nation

'I consider myself to have been unbelievably lucky in being so deeply involved in the showband world. I enjoyed every second of it and was even paid to do it.'

Declan Ryan, the Regal showband

To counteract the increasing attraction and popularity of English television – which could only be accessed in Dublin and along Ireland's east coast – and in an effort to prevent the dilution of Irish culture, life and attitudes, the Irish government took the decision in 1960 to set up the national television service, Telefís Éireann. It was scheduled to go on air at Christmas 1961, but Eamonn Andrews took the strange decision to give the organisation the Christmas off. It finally began transmitting at 7pm on New Year's Eve, 1961. It was received with a great sense of pride and was welcomed nationally. The new service was enormously popular and had a profound

THE NEVADA SHOWBAND

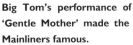

Big Tom's performance of 'Gentle Mother' made the Mainliners famous.

effect on Irish life and entertainment in general, and on the showbands in particular. While national radio had been a boon and a blessing since 1926, and had filled a great need, particularly in the remote and rural areas, this latest venture was a different ball game altogether, bringing a whole new dimension into Irish life. It has to be remembered that nearly ninety percent of the Irish population had no access whatsoever to television prior to this, so this was real innovation and progress. Even the newsreaders became stars and it was reported that people 'dressed up' for the news, so that the dapper Charles Mitchell would see them looking their best!

Programme planners quickly realised that in the showbands they had a very saleable, homegrown commodity with nationwide appeal. Before long, some of the top bands had made their first tentative TV appearances. And then the hour-long TV spectacular, 'The Showband Show', made its debut on the nation's screens in June of 1963. It was compèred by Paul Russell. The show was an instant success and soon became compulsive viewing for a great many people. It ran for almost two years, projecting the showbands into people's homes even in the remotest parts of Ireland. This was undreamed-of exposure for the bands and introduced them to a new and vast audience – the non-dancers. What made the show unique was that the atmosphere in the studio was very relaxed (as TV programmes go). The featured band was not restricted in any way by the production teams, but had the freedom to play their choice of programme, their way. This approach brought the best out of the bands, just like at a live dance. The formula was a resounding success and bands pulled out all the stops to try and get a slot on the show.

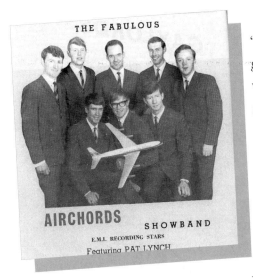

THE FABULOUS

AIRCHORDS SHOWBAND

E.M.I. RECORDING STARS

Featuring PAT LYNCH

The Saints made their appearance on 'The Showband Show' on 1 January 1965 – a great beginning to the new year. I remember we chose a varied but safe and familiar programme, which included 'Yesterday Man', 'Ring of Fire', Billy J Kramer's 'Little Children', the Jim Reeves standard 'I Love You Because', and 'To Whom It Concerns' – later to become famous as the intro music to 'The Late Late Show' – and a couple of big brass numbers. For my sins, I sang a Hank Williams song, 'Those Wedding Bells Will Never Ring For Me'. I don't recall being nervous or anything like that, but there was excitement and anticipation. It was all very new to us.

Here we were, preparing to perform to three cameramen: 'That was perfect – we'll just run through it five more times to be safe!' This vote of confidence came from the man known as the Floor Manager, complete with receiver in his left ear and a direct line to God through a walkie-talkie in his right hand. God in this case was the producer, who I now know was Adrian Cronin. Finally it was, as they say in television, 'in the can', and I am happy to say that we were pleased with our performance. I am not for a second suggesting that we were the finished, polished product – far from it – but we were lively and honest, smiled a lot and were musically adept, and it came across well.

A spot on 'The Showband Show' was considered a great coup for any band, but more particularly if the band was not well established, as it gave you

Dermot O'Brien and the Clubmen. The accordion virtuoso had a big hit with 'The Merry Ploughboy'.

considerable leverage with promoters when negotiating future booking fees. It was national exposure, and brought great prestige and almost an assurance of success – if you made the most of your chance. The mighty Mainliners from Castleblaney were one band that grabbed it with both hands. They were just another average band until Tom McBride sang a number called 'Gentle Mother' on the show. The song made a great impact on viewers and overnight the band became known nationally. As a result they packed ballrooms wherever they played and took off in a very big way. 'Big Tom' became a household name and one of the biggest draws in the business. He is singing and recording to this day.

Larry Cunningham & The Mighty Avons

Souvenir: The Ohio Showband

16. No Dancing Please, It's Lent!

'Having a potential No. 1 record banned in Ireland for political purposes convinced me that my only way of getting to the top was to continue erecting the TV aerial masts.'
Joe Flynn, the Saints

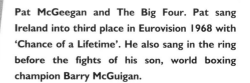

Pat McGeegan and The Big Four. Pat sang Ireland into third place in Eurovision 1968 with 'Chance of a Lifetime'. He also sang in the ring before the fights of his son, world boxing champion Barry McGuigan.

The Catholic Church has always been a powerful influence on all aspects of Irish life, so much so that in 1951 *The Irish Times*, in response to the resignation of Dr Noel Browne over the Mother and Child Scheme, was moved to write: 'The most serious revelation is that the Roman Catholic Church would seem to be the effective government of this country.' It has to be said that a lot of the Church's influence was good and meant for the best, but in the entertainment business it had a stifling effect. For years it controlled and monitored the dancing of perfectly decent people in rural parish halls and strictly enforced a ban on all dancing during the seven-week season of Lent.

Local councillor Eugene McMenamen recalls of Strabane's Pallidrome ballroom days: 'By the late 'fifties the social climate was changing rapidly. When ballrooms sprang up, they threatened the parish dances and many parishioners will remember Fr Convey standing outside St Mary's Hall in Bridge

Street, making sure that if you were on your way to the Pallidrome you didn't get there, as he diverted you into the parish hall. However, this only lasted a short while because the excitement of Ireland's top showbands playing in the Pallidrome offered too much.'

Apart from the Lenten fast and abstinence promoted and practised at the time, any form of amusement or entertainment was frowned on and dancing was not allowed from Ash Wednesday to Easter Sunday. The one exception was Ireland's national holiday, St Patrick's Day, on 17 March, which generally fell in the middle of Lent. It is not difficult to imagine the Irish celebrating this one holiday to the full. In the midst of enforced abstinence, more than a few 'jars' were consumed and the dancers made full use of the opportunity to 'doll up', dance and enjoy themselves. The bands also eagerly awaited the chance for one big gig during the imposed lay-off. I can well remember my own impatience to play, having rehearsed new and fresh numbers and knowing that a huge crowd was assured wherever you played on St Patrick's night.

There was, however, another side to the equation – that of the professional musicians who depended totally on performing music for their livelihood. Scant attention was paid to their predicament. For seven weeks there were no bookings and consequently no money. They felt increasingly hard done by as they were required to tighten their belts and the traditional large Irish families were left to wonder why their breadwinner failed to provide over the long season of Lent. The hall owners and promoters were, of course, equally unhappy with the situation, but nevertheless they all complied with tradition – all except one.

A dance was advertised in a small country hall in the midlands during Lent. The venue was an instant sell-out, having no competition whatsoever. The local clergy were incensed and stood at the entrance to the hall to coerce and threaten the punters,

The Michael O'Callaghan Big Band, from Buttevant. Their record, 'Cuando Sali De Cuba', was banned.

LATEST and GREATEST RELEASE!

BROKEN-HEARTED FARMER FEATURING

JOE with the SAINTS showband ATHLONE

c/w "OLD BOG ROAD" on Tribune Label

BUY IT NOW!

Joe Flynn, on right of picture, comforts a broken-hearted farmer.

some of whom were decried from the church pulpit.

It has to be remembered that these people were from a tight-knit community and well known to each other – there was no anonymity. At that time the clergy were very powerful and respected and, in general, people did not openly cross them. However the dam was now breached and soon other venues tentatively followed suit. The dancers plucked up their courage and supported the venues. The initial trickle became a flood and soon there was no going back.

The petty and restrictive practices of those days was further in evidence in some of the decisions taken by Radio Éireann, the national broadcasting corporation. When Pat McGeegan (father of boxing champion Barry McGuigan) recorded a fine version of 'The Wedding', the record was banned from the airwaves simply because the lyrics contained the words 'Ave Maria' (Hail Mary). It was considered by the establishment to be in poor taste. Surely the population were sensible enough and intelligent enough to decide for themselves? In any case, the same song – word for word – was available on a recording by Julie Rogers.

During the farmers' protest in 1966, the Saints released a record called 'The Broken-Hearted Farmer'. It featured Joe Flynn, with topical lyrics penned by his wife Mary. Although sympathetic to the farmers' stance, it 'told it like it was'. The record launched promisingly enough until the farmers'

The Saints give Macra na Feirme a preview of 'The Broken-Hearted Farmer'. The late TJ Maher MEP is standing (right).

protest gathered momentum and tractors and lorries blocked the bridge over the Shannon. I can well remember this causing chaos, as the main artery to the west of Ireland was effectively sealed. Politics raised its head. Pressure was brought to bear and, without explanation, our record was banned.

The Broken-Hearted Farmer (Lyrics by Mary Flynn)

Sure it is poor we are today, and we'll always be that way
Even though we're trying hard to get a hearing
For the prices are too low and it's up they'll have to go
Or the farmer will be left all broken-hearted

Twas in the year of '66 that we took our brogues and sticks
And joined the men from Cork and started walking
But it was to no avail we sat down against the rails
And refused to budge until they started talking

Acushla geal ma croí, won't you listen to our plea
And you'll have the prayers of broken-hearted farmers
Sure we sold both cheap and low, now it's time we had more dough
So we started our campaign and went-a-marching

In another instance of censorship, a super record on the Honey label, performed by the Michael O'Callaghan Big Band from Buttevant, County Cork, was banned. The song, 'Cuando Sali De Cuba' (When I left Cuba), had some very effective, simple brass figures and was sung beautifully by Eleanor Nodwell, whom I met up with years later when she sang with the Syd Laurence Orchestra. In a *Spotlight* magazine review at the time, Larry Gogan praised the record, which he said was very well performed. He added: 'I'd love to see it in the charts, because it has a touch of class.' It didn't have much chance of that when it couldn't get airplay. I never found out the reason for the ban.

People had spent money recording, pressing and promoting these records and I can only think that today, in all three cases, there would certainly be grounds for litigation. The Irish are an educated people and in the intervening years we have seen those in a position of power become more reasonable, more enlightened and more sensible. At least, I hope so.

17. The Carnival: Mud and Summer Magic

O ne of the unique features of Irish summer life in the 'sixties was the local carnival. Apart from the well-known national festivals like Puck Fair and the Rose of Tralee, most small towns and villages also held and celebrated their own carnival, the highlight of which was fourteen consecutive night of dancing, featuring a different showband each night. The event was widely publicised and generated a lot of interest, both locally and from further afield. The dance posters, big and brightly painted, screamed out at you from the sides of country roads

A great line-up of bands for Puck Fair.

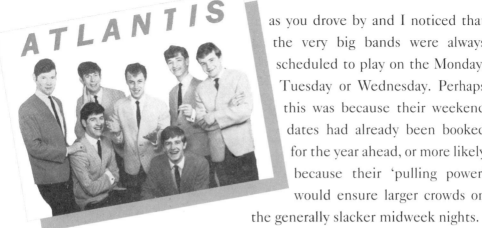

as you drove by and I noticed that the very big bands were always scheduled to play on the Monday, Tuesday or Wednesday. Perhaps this was because their weekend dates had already been booked for the year ahead, or more likely because their 'pulling power' would ensure larger crowds on the generally slacker midweek nights.

The dances were held in five-pole marquees, which were supposed to remain cool and comfortable on hot summer evenings. Believe me, this was not always the case. Facilities were very primitive, and if it rained a lot the whole area could quickly turn into a quagmire. Trudging through four inches of mud to pay your five bob admission fee was not the best prelude to an evening's dancing and certainly did nothing for your treasured new shoes or nylon stockings. However, at a good carnival, on the right balmy night, dancing to a good showband was a memory that would last forever. The marquees could hold crowds of 2,000 plus, but with the right band and the right weather the turnout very often exceeded this number. A great rivalry grew up between the bands as dancers had an opportunity to hear and compare different bands on consecutive nights. Crowd attendances were gauged, the merits of different 'line-ups' and their choices of programme were discussed at length and inevitably a league table of bands began to develop. Some hardened punters went to hear all fourteen showbands.

A common sight we would encounter on our way to these venues was fifteen or twenty cyclists, peddling furiously on their way to the

The Black Aces, from Kilkenny. Jimmy Lennon later played with me in New City Sounds.

dance, shouting and waving merrily to you as you passed in the bandwagon. They generally came and made themselves known to you after the dance and had the chat.

The carnival marquee was also home to what we in the business affectionately called a 'scout'. He was that breed of 'over-the-top' showband fan who you could expect to meet at any dance within a sixty-mile radius of his home town, especially at carnivals. He was an agreeable, disarming type of fellow who would approach you before or after the dance as if he knew you all your life. He never missed a dance, although he never danced. He was invariably alone, taking stock of your performance from start to finish. He was a mine of information on all the bands, and could tell you who was 'hot' or who was on the slide, which lead guitarist was leaving which band and who the replacement was going to be. He knew the band that had new stage-wear, which band was going on tour or who was about to record. It was only afterwards that you realised he had been pumping you for information about your own band throughout the whole conversation. Whenever he was spotted, the message would jokingly come across the bandstand as you played, 'Watch out for your man, he's a scout.' He was a harmless and colourful part of the scene, and I suspect that there was no ulterior motive behind his actions; he simply got a buzz out of feeling that he had the inside track on the showbands and felt that he shared in the excitement of the whole thing.

Left: the Cadets, one of the most colourful bands of the period! Great sound, great outfits. Above: Frankie McDonald and myself did a stint with the Central Seven showband, from Offaly, before becoming Saints.

18. The Border and the Miami Tragedy

In the early 1960s the border between the Republic and Northern Ireland was more of an irritant than a threat to the showbands, who regularly criss-crossed it from both sides without giving it a second thought. You did, however, have to get your closing music right – either 'The Soldiers Song' or 'God Save the Queen', depending on where you were playing. It was one of those decisions where there was no room for error.

Consider the scenario: a band in the South receives a billing to play in a small town in the North, let's say Lisnaskee, and nobody in the band is quite sure 'which leg they kick with' in the particular vicinity of the hall. Now, what religion the band or the dancers were didn't matter at all to either side, and the dancers certainly didn't care where the band came from as long as they had a good night. What did matter was that the band, having given them a good night, finished with the 'right' anthem.

On arrival at the hall there would be a discreet search for clues – for example, a picture of the Queen, Winston Churchill or a union jack. A picture of the Pope or a tricolour would be equally convincing for the other side. Armed with indisputable evidence, the choice was made, the correct tune was played and

I can never remember any cases of 'mistaken identity'. The northern bands enjoyed coming south and looked forward to it. In fact there were many northern musicians playing in bands in the South, and vice versa. There was more trouble in Glasgow than in Northern Ireland in those days.

One of the plusses of going north was that musical instruments were much cheaper in Northern Ireland. It wasn't always easy to get them back through the customs and excise people who manned the border crossing points, but I know lots who did. Eventually we were required to carry a manifesto of equipment, detailing instrument serial numbers and so on, which had to be presented at border posts. On the way home in the early hours of the morning there might be a random check on a selected instrument. Looking back on it now, it seems to me that when this happened there was always snow on the ground and the chosen instrument always happened to be the first loaded, thereby requiring all the gear to be offloaded onto the side of the road to get at it. It was annoying, but the events of 31 July, 1975 put all the annoyance and irritation into stark perspective.

As the Miami showband returned from a gig at the Castle ballroom, Bambridge, at around 2am, they were flagged down at what they assumed was a security checkpoint. What followed sent shockwaves throughout the showband world and shatterered the cosy perception that bands and musicians were somehow outside the tragedy that Northern Ireland had become. The uniformed 'security' roadblock had been set up by the Ulster Volunteer Force (UVF), a Protestant, loyalist organisation. The five band members in the minibus were a mix of Catholics and Protestants, which was certainly not uncommon at the time. They were not overly concerned at being stopped, as musicians crossing the border were used to random checks by the

Tony Geraghty   Fran O'Toole   Brian McCoy

security forces. Then they were ordered to line up by the roadside and place their hands on their heads while their names and addresses were being taken. Unknown to the musicians, two of the terrorists were busy placing a bomb in the rear of the van. Stephen Travers, the bass player and most recent band member, saw them rummaging among the band gear, took down his hands and demanded to know what they were doing with his guitar.

Suddenly the world erupted as the bomb exploded prematurely, instantly killing both terrorists. Panic ensued. Travers, who had been thrown in the air by the blast, was then shot in the hip, the bullet travelling upwards and puncturing his lung. His colleagues Fran O'Toole, Tony Geraghty and Brian McCoy fell dead in a hail of machine-gun fire. In the confusion, Des Lee managed to escape. He ran across a field and flagged down a passing truck, which took him to Newry police station.

News of the killings shocked Miami fans throughout the country and traumatised everyone in the extended showband community. The loss was senseless and inexplicable. Northern Ireland became a no-go area for a lot of the showbands. Another innocent business fell victim to terrorism and the demise of an already ailing industry was inevitably hastened.

Subsequently, four men were convicted and received life sentences for their parts in the Miami atrocity.

19. The English Tour

'I was playing the showband gigs in England in Lent, which gave me the chance on nights off to go down to the Marquee and see the Yardbirds or Spencer Davis.'
Rory Gallagher

The Lenten ban, which I mentioned earlier, did have one positive spin-off – it started the trend of the English tour, opening up a whole new audience to the showbands. In order to earn a living during the seven-week barren period at home, bands were driven to cross the water in search of bookings. They found work in the Irish clubs and ballrooms of England, where they were welcomed with open arms.

The arrival of the Irish showbands was a wonderful bonus to the vast numbers of Irish exiles now working in Britain. At the time, there was unlimited work on the building and demolition sites, as Britain rebuilt, following the bombing raids and devastation of the war. Irish workers filled the 'bedsitter--land' of every major English city. With very little to do in the 'digs' that were the normal accommodation of the Irish exile, the clubs became a beacon – a haven in which to socialise, to catch up with news from home, to chat, to drink and to dance. Most of these clubs also did sterling welfare work when the need arose.

The Irish who mingled so closely together in the clubs came from every county in Ireland – with different football loyalties, different hurling loyalties

The innovative Chessmen. Bass player Bobby Ballagh (second from right) achieved fame as an artist and designer.

and different showband loyalties – all of which generated a great, good-natured rivalry. It was a very different scenario from the security of their home counties back in Ireland, with their own familiar accents and allegiances.

The showbands' success was immediate. They played music that the emigrants recognised and loved. They were a nostalgic link with home, especially if a band happened to come from your own particular county. The clubs were packed to the doors. So successful were these Lenten tours that many bands began to go back three and four times a year. A pattern became established: depart from Dublin; sail (as the wagon and equipment had to be transported) into Liverpool and play the Irish Centre there; then on to Manchester's Astoria or Ard Rí Club; Birmingham's Harp or Shamrock Club; Coventry's Banba Club or the Locarno; and then Luton and a week playing the London clubs. We would usually play the same route back to Liverpool and home. On one of our very early tours, we discovered that the agent had made only three bookings out of the twelve promised – the final nine bookings had never been confirmed. Worse still, as there had been so much hype in the local papers before we left, with full-page spreads and so on, we dared not risk the embarrassment of going home until the fortnight was up. So, I confess, we stayed in London instead, tightened our belts and watched our pennies!

One of our most enjoyable single-venue gigs was the Astoria (later the Carousel) in Manchester. We would generally fly out on the Friday morning, be collected at the airport and play the club on Friday, Saturday and Sunday nights. There was a very competent resident band – the Internationals –

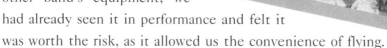

who played till midnight, and we would then perform until 2am. It had been arranged for us to use the resident band's stage equipment, and although most bands would be reluctant to use another band's equipment, we had already seen it in performance and felt it was worth the risk, as it allowed us the convenience of flying.

This popular club was one of the Bill Fuller chain, very efficiently run by Peggy and Peter McCabe, and always thronged. For us it was virtually a weekend break, apart from the two hours a night playing, which we enjoyed anyway. There was no setting up or stripping down of equipment, no constant travelling, and we took full advantage of the football at Old Trafford, the amusement park at Belle View and the attractions of Manchester's Piccadilly.

The DIXIES Showband - Cork

Among the London clubs that were most popular with the Irish, and therefore with the showbands, were the Galtymore in Cricklewood, the Gresham on Holloway Road, the Hibernian in Fulham Broadway, the Shandon in Romford in Essex and the Buffalo in Camden Town. These played host to every Irish nurse who ever studied or practised in London, as well as to every major showband that ever aspired to make music. The Gresham boasted a revolving stage, very novel in those days. While the resident band played to the crowd at the front, we set up at the rear. When it was time for us to play, the stage would slowly revolve, bearing one band away and bringing on the next. One of my early and abiding memories of the Gresham was of being introduced as 'the big band from Ireland' (remember, there were eight of us), and of rotating into view playing 'Ring of Fire' as the crowd cheered its approval. This introduction and reception was made all the stranger by the fact that the resident house band, who were disappearing backstage, were musically superb and boasted eighteen members.

The Hibernian in Fulham had the rather daunting tradition of requiring the showband stars to perform, unaccompanied, for the management and bar staff after each gig. To their credit, they all rose to the challenge.

Incidentally, a young lad helping out backstage in those days was none other than Shamus Moore, who was later to establish himself as a fine Irish entertainer all over England with his infectious hit 'The Yellow JCB'. He must have picked up a lot of musical tips from the bands in his time at the Gresham.

20. The Digs: An Education

The accommodation – the 'digs' – used by bands on tour in the early days would merit a book all to themselves. Hotels were not within our budget, so the digs were pretty basic, but as the first tour was often also a band's first trip outside Ireland, and as many bands came from small towns in Ireland and were used to 'roughing it', most were not disposed to complain. It was part of the excitement and novelty of the whole thing.

Who will ever forget Seven Sisters Road, Finsbury Park, and a certain famous, or should I say infamous, establishment, which catered for touring bands in the early 'sixties? Fellow guests when we stayed there in 1965 included the Impact showband from Cork, featuring Rory Gallagher, who were on tour in London at the time. Any non-musician in the house was referred to as a 'normal'. The proprietor did not like 'normals', as he would be required to rise early and prepare breakfast for them. In fact, looking back at it, it seems astonishing that any 'normals' would have wanted to stay in an establishment that catered for musicians. The very nature of the band business, with dances finishing at 2am or 3am, dictated that you had musicians coming in noisily at all hours. Consideration for those already in bed was certainly not their most pressing concern. The bands had no set breakfast time. As individuals arose they simply went to the kitchen and cooked their own. I suppose, in hindsight, it was the ideal set-up.

The relaxed wake-up times had their disadvantages, however. It was not uncommon in those days to leave the band gear set up after a gig and for a rehearsal to be scheduled for early the following morning. It was a good idea – if the whole band showed up. One bandleader, fed up with persistent absentees, introduced a £5 fine for offenders. It was enough to get most of the reluctant risers up. However, the story is told of a well-known trumpet player who was late once too often and finally provoked the irate bandleader into storming to the offender's hotel room, where he found the musician snoring soundly and a £5 note pinned to the foot of the bed!

I have a vivid recollection of being woken by a full-scale rehearsal on the second floor at five o'clock one morning. On investigation it transpired that a London-based group had had an argument at their gig and decided to disband. They were selling their entire PA system and the prospective buyers, there and then, had insisted on a full-scale demonstration of the rig. As you can imagine, power and volume was a vital requirement in any sound system and I can vouch that these were certainly being tested to the limit, regardless of the hour or the eardrums of the other occupants. 'Select' and 'classy' were never descriptions appropriate to our accommodation at that time. On later tours we became a little bit choosier and the standard of accommodation improved accordingly, but whether it was as much fun is debatable.

Although in theory and according to the proprietor, all the rooms in whatever accommodation we booked were 'the best rooms', everyone knew that some were better than others and there was intense competition to get the choice few. Some band members, like the proverbial holidaying

First of the NEW WAVE—

IMPACT Showband CORK

Manager— J. Philip Prendergast Phone Cork 20140

The beginnings of a legend: Rory Gallagher (third from left) in his showband days.

TOM DUNPHY

Above: Tom Dunphy of the Royal had a smash hit with 'If I Didn't Have a Dime'.

Germans with their beach towels, always seemed to get there first. All sorts of stunts were pulled to delay the competition – mysterious phone calls at the reception desk, suitcases that got 'hidden' amongst the band gear, so that by the time the hapless 'mark' had finally got himself sorted, the best rooms were long gone and he would once again be over the laundry or in a broom cupboard beside the lift. It was all part of the 'craic'.

Free time in the afternoons was generally spent browsing the music shops in the West End, listening to the afternoon bands at the Lyceum, swimming or playing football in Finsbury Park.

Green Angels

21. The Irish Recording Industry

'In 1963 we were known as the Red Devils, playing around in the third division, with Joe wishing he could be Brendan Bowyer and me wishing I could be TJ Byrne. In 1964 we recorded our first record, 'The Answer to Everything', and within four weeks we were playing in the first division, drawing thousands of people. I didn't have enough vacant dates to play all the venues that wanted to book us.'
Seamus Casey, Manager of Joe Dolan and the Drifters

Declan Ryan, who had a big hit with 'I Need You'.

For the first of the showbands there was no recording facility at all available in Ireland, and some of the pioneering bands, like the Clipper Carlton, never recorded. When a facility did come, in the early 'sixties, it was unbelievably basic and low-tech, even by the standards of the time. A small room at 40 Henry Street, Dublin, with a single-track tape recorder and a radio producer named Bill O'Donovan, was 'the business'. The very first Irish-produced records reflected the quality of the equipment and had a rawness and honesty about them that was a million miles away from today's sanitised, high-tech and digitised offerings. All credit to the pathfinders

**One of the early
recording studios was based in Parnell Square.**

for having a go, even if the results were less than mind-blowing. The punters, however, were either very forgiving or simply didn't notice, accepting the results eagerly and without complaint. They were simply glad that they could now listen to their homegrown showband stars, produced by an Irish producer in an Irish studio, in their own home. However you looked at it, this was progress.

As demand for studio time slowly increased, recording studios modernised – new multi-track equipment came online, string sections were introduced where necessary, results improved and the industry raced ahead as more and more bands recorded. Silverpine and the Eamon Andrews studios built a solid reputation for decent-quality recordings, and both became very popular with recording bands. Nobody at the time made a fortune from actual record sales, as the whole exercise was targeted at the ballroom box office. If you had a record that was getting airplay, it promoted the band nationwide, which brought punters through the ballroom doors, led to increased bookings and was a lever to negotiate a better percentage of the takings. Needless to say, the vast majority of records sank without trace. However, there were some successes and those that 'hit', such as Dickie Rock's 'Candy Store' or Joe Dolan's 'The Answer to Everything', became huge and even today remain part of the showband legacy.

Ireland's Top 20

ALL THE TOP 20 AND OTHER RECORDS Available from McHugh Himself 39 TALBOT STREET, DUBLIN 1. Records Posted To Any Address.

A SPELL BINDER "HEIDSCHI BUMBEIDSCHI" By DANA

'FUNNY GIRL' BY Barbra Streisand ON CBS

WATCH INDIAN LAKE BY THE MEMORIES

'GREAT BALLS OF FIRE' BY TINY TIM ON PYE

LAST WEEK	THIS WEEK	
1	1	QUICK JOEY SMALL—Real McCoy
4	2	OB-LA-DI, OB-LA-DA—The Marmalade
5	3	BUILD ME UP BUTTERCUP—The Foundations
3	4	LILY THE PINK—Scaffold
7	5	A MINUTE OF YOUR TIME—Tom Jones
8	6	KATIES KISSES—Dixies
11	7	MY LOVELY ROSE & YOU —Sean Fagan and the Pacific
12	8	I'M A TIGER—Lulu
14	9	ALBATROSS—Fleetwood Mac
2	10	CHRISTMAS POLKA—The Hoedowners
6	11	THE GOOD, THE BAD AND THE UGLY —Hugo Montenegro
9	12	ONE TWO THREE, O'LEARY — Des O'Connor
18	13	ATLANTIS—Donovan
19	14	LOVE CHILD—Supremes
10	15	AIN'T GOT NO, I GOT LIFE—Nina Simone
—	16	SOMETHING'S HAPPENING — Hermans Hermits
13	17	ELEANOR—The Turtles
16	18	NEVER AN EVERYDAY THING —Granny's Intentions
20	19	I DON'T WANT TO BE A MEMORY —Pattersons
17	20	THE GREAT EL TIGRE —Larry Cunningham

This *Spotlight* chart
shows that the showbands were able to hold their
own with the big names. The Real McCoy, the Dixies, the Pacific, the
Hoedowners and Larry Cunningham all feature in the top twenty.

English recording companies eventually woke up to the existence of this hugely untapped showband market and became involved. I remember a recording session with the Saints in a cellar in Parnell Square, Dublin, for Irish Records Factors in April 1965. The session was sponsored by Decca Records and engineered from a trailer parked outside the building, while we recorded in the cellar inside. The producer was Peter Sullivan – the man who turned down the Beatles ('We don't like their music and anyway guitar music is on the way out' – Decca Recording Company, on rejecting the Beatles in 1962). Sullivan also produced records for Tom Jones and Englebert Humperdink. During our session he was a stickler for diction and insisted on each number being first sung into his ear, totally unaccompanied, before starting to record.

I managed to sell one track I had written, 'Tell Me You Love Me', to Burlington Music Company in London, and it was later released in Australasia. I received some royalties, but have to admit that I was not able to retire on the proceeds.

The success of Eurovision records such as Butch Moore's 1965 hit 'Walking the Streets in the Rain', penned by Phil Coulter, further enhanced the business and by the mid-1960s the Irish record charts were displaying as many home-produced Irish showband hits as foreign imports. It was a remarkable achievement in a few short years. It was good for the bands, good for the business and good for the country. From this modest start, which of us back then could have predicted where the Irish music business was heading? Certainly we could not have envisaged the lofty position it holds worldwide today, with multimillion sellers such as U2, Enya, the Corrs, Sinead O'Connor, Van Morrison, etc. I am reminded that 'a journey of a thousand miles begins with a single step' and in this case it was the showbands who took that first step.

22. The American Tour: Another World

As can be imagined, the opportunity of travelling to and touring the United States in the early 'sixties was too good a chance to pass up. In fact, if the truth was to be told, most of us would have done it for nothing, but we did not say no to the few shillings. Generally the tour was to the eastern seaboard and as a rule took in New York, Boston, Chicago and Washington, all areas with large Irish communities. On our first US tour, we flew out of Shannon and spent the entire three weeks in New York. The Monarchs, from Limerick, were on the same flight. They had been booked by Bill Fuller, a wealthy Kerryman who had chains of ballrooms in both

Tommy Drennan began as a boy soprano, and was noted for his fine voice throughout his career.

Tina of the Mexicans, who later joined the Real McCoy.

the USA and England. Needless to say, we teamed up on board for a laugh and a jar or two.

On landing at JFK, we were surprised to be met by officials from the American Federation of Musicians union (AFM). They demanded that we employ, and pay, an equal number of their members as there were of us to play on the tour with us. We were working the tour for a Kerry exile named Timmy Moynihan, who was persuaded to agree. This of course cut our playing times in half, as we shared the four-hour gigs with the American band, who were led by an Irish-American named Johnny O'Neill. Johnny turned out to be more Irish than any of us, in thought, word and deed. We hit it off immediately and, after the first weekend, he insisted that we all move out of the hotel and stay in his house. This we did, and it started a lifelong friendship. I recall that we only worked the weekends – Friday, Saturday and Sunday. We always found the American-Irish good-natured, welcoming, open and hospitable to a fault.

Being used to the low-key local poster and newspaper advertising in Ireland, the hype in America was a real eye-opener. We were extensively promoted and advertised on radio and billboards, with great emphasis on the 'direct from Ireland' line. I can remember travelling up the New York State highway in an open-top Cadillac, listening to the radio announcer tell the world how good we were. The truth is we were not too bad. Wisely, we had altered our programme slightly for the American audience, to include a touch of nostalgia, home and emigration. We played numbers like 'Galway Bay', 'Danny Boy' and 'Where the River Shannon Flows'. We got a great reception in the clubs – the Ambassador in Queens, the Red Mill in the Bronx, Jaegar House – and in our final week we enjoyed a thirty percent crowd increase.

The hospitality shown to us was unbelievable, and we were given the full tour: the Empire State Building, the Statue of Liberty, Broadway, Rockaway Beach, even Harlem. Four of us were taken up New York State to the Catskill Mountains, to stay at Shamrock House from the Monday to the Friday morning. Of course, even there, music was played and songs were sung. And all this hospitality came from total strangers, who had taken a week off work to play host to us. It was dreamlike, unreal and unforgettable. n 1965 we went twice. Happy days!

DICKIE ROCK
OF THE MIAMI SHOWBAND

THE CAPITOLS

WITH BUTCH MOORE

23. Expanding Horizons: Hunt Balls and Air Force Bases

In my view, the greatest mistake that Irish showbands made in England was not to capitalise on their opportunity and take the next, and, to me, obvious step – to expand their horizons by moving away from the Irish clubs. Perhaps they felt that it was enough to have a regular circuit and steady, well-paying work, but they were playing to the converted again and again. They failed to see where the future lay – the big league: the English Mecca ballroom circuit, the English clubs, the hunt balls, the universities and the American Air Force bases. They could and would have been a sensation. At that time, these venues were being fed a diet of four-piece groups (three guitars and drums), with nothing like the power of seven- or eight-piece showbands with their brass, variety and talent. It would have been no contest. But it did not happen. Fifteen years after their first tour, the showbands were still playing the selfsame Irish venues.

In 1967 I decided to spread my wings a little. The decline in the showband scene in Ireland was becoming apparent so, with great regrets and lots of fond memories, I parted amicably from the Saints and emigrated to Coventry in England. Not long afterwards I was invited to become bandleader of New

Las Vegas – my Coventry-based showband.

City Sounds, with whom I played for four great years, including a number of appearances on 'Opportunity Knocks'. At the time I was also working for Rolls Royce engineering.

In 1971 there were distinct signs that the showband boom in the Irish halls in Britain, which were our main venues, was coming to an end. I was convinced that the English scene presented a much wider and untapped potential for the showband sound and was concerned that, despite our wins on 'Opportunity Knocks', we were still playing the same old venues. So I gave in my notice at New City Sounds, and set about forming the Las Vegas showband. We would boldly go where no showband had gone before!

I had the line-up all mapped out in my head. Now all I had to do was ask the musicians. I approached a bass player by the name of Bill Dodd, a solid guy with a great singing voice. His first question was, 'Who have we got?' to which I replied honestly, 'You, I hope.' He looked at me a bit strangely, then I mentioned the other names I had in mind and he said, 'Count me in.' Within a week, the seven-piece band had been assembled and a month later we played our first gig, at the Moonrakers club in Swindon. The band was musically adept, with a very good brass section, and looked well on stage, but there was no projection, no 'show' and no choreography. So it was back to basics and to the proven showband formula. We made sure our programme was varied. While we covered the major pop hits of the time, I did not want to become recognised as just another pop band. So we set about seriously rehearsing seven or eight production numbers, such as 'The Dambusters March', to which we added the intercom sequence and explosion sounds from the film in the last chorus. It was very effective, and extremely popular on the RAF club circuit. We also did a Spike Jones routine that included gunshots, klaxons, whistles, hooters, etc. All of this demanded precise timing, but the crowd re-action was well worth the effort. Other regulars were 'The Laughing Police-man' and the 'Posthorn Gallop', in which we used an actual posthorn. We also featured the theme from 'The Power Game', and the brass section would play from the back of the hall or from the Chairman's box, which gave the number more impact. These numbers were intended to complement a strong and var-ied dancing programme and to ensure that the band was remembered and, hopefully, rebooked. It seemed to work.

It was a brave decision – to forego the steady work, to branch out into the unknown. But we need not have worried. From four-hour stints on the Irish circuit, we were surprised to suddenly find that our required playing times were now only two one-hour spots – at a stroke condensing our already good programme to our very best numbers. Promoters were impressed by our work rate, variety and ability. The show, faithfully based on the Irish showband tra-dition, was different and colourful. Our finisher, 'The Holy City', became something of an anthem on our regular club circuit, with the punters standing on tables and chairs, singing along enthusiastically. The word spread. Book-ings rolled in – from universities, American Air Force bases, hunt balls, the Showmen's Guild, the Round Table, chambers of commerce and debs balls. There was an element of cloak-and-dagger activity on some of the debs gigs, as the venue was kept secret – even from the band. The arrangement was that we were to be met at a given time at a specified service area on the motorway, and then follow our contact to the venue. It turned out that these measures were designed to deter gatecrashers.

I am a firm believer in trying to personalise a function in some way. For ex-ample, when we were booked to do a large Italian gathering in Birmingham one night, I put together a quick arrangement of their national anthem and we started the show with it. As the curtains opened, the crowd, which in-cluded grandparents, babes-in-arms and all ages in between, came to their feet with hands on hearts and began to sing. We could do no wrong for the rest of the evening.

The American Air Force bases in the UK were a particularly lucrative source of bookings. The bases themselves were virtual tracts of America on British soil and every single commodity on them – from beer to sugar sachets –

was flown in from the States. The currency used was US dollars, so you always ended up after the gig with a pocketful of dimes and quarters. I would try to discover the squadron or regimental march of any Air Force or Army base we played and include it in the evening's programme. One night I was approached after a private function and booked for the NCOs' summer ball at Bramcote Barracks. The man doing the asking was Jim Hamilton, the Regimental Sergeant Major. He explained that they were Hussars, a cavalry regiment who wore spurs on dress occasions, and that we had played their regimental tune, the Posthorn Gallop, during our show that night. It was enough to ensure three dates a year with them. When he was promoted and transferred to Germany, he even had us flown out to do his summer ball in Hohne. He had organised ten bookings for us and we were wined and dined and put up in his Mess for the duration. I later found out that for official records we were Alvis engineers checking out their armoured vehicle engines! We soon became well established on the RAF bases. When I would get an enquiry for a big night like the Battle of Britain Ball, I would agree on condition that we got to play the Officers' Mess on the Friday night and the NCOs' Mess on the Saturday night. This would work out great for us, as accommodation would be arranged and all our meals provided in the Mess. It cut our travelling expenses in half and saved on hotel bills.

As Wednesday was the military's payday, it was a big night for entertainment. Showbands were normally booked for an hour's dancing before and after the floorshow. The floorshow was always composed of American acts provided by the American government to tour their bases overseas, and we often found ourselves on the bill with the likes of the Three Degrees, Johnny Cash, the Equals and Del Shannon. Sometimes we were called on to perform

PRESSED STEEL FISHER (Cowley) SPORTS & SOCIAL CLUB

ROMANWAY
EMPEROR BALLROOM

Saturday, 15th December
8 p.m. to midnight

THE POPULAR BAND
OF YOUR CHOICE :—

THE
LAS VEGAS SHOWBAND
Leader : Barry O'Keefe

MEMBERS 50p.   GUESTS 60p.
ON SALE 12th NOVEMBER

Oliver & Son (Oxford) Ltd.

at the Airmen's Club and the NCOs' Club on the one night, which could have been a nightmare for an unprepared band. Our first appearance at a US Airmen's Club was a very sharp learning curve, and a very uncomfortable experience. Ten minutes into the show the crowd, who were mostly young and mostly black, began to shout, 'We want soul, man, give us some soul.' The truth is, we did not have one soul number. There was nothing we could do but try to smile through what became a very long and embarrassing spot. Believe me, our next rehearsal contained a lot of soul. But we got our stripes back at the NCOs' Club that same night. Jimmy Lennon, our lead vocalist at the time, had played with the Black Aces from Kilkenny. He was an exceptional performer, particularly at rock 'n' roll numbers, and would often jump down to join the crowds dancing around the stage. The NCOs loved him, and for the rest of the show the crowd kept shouting to me, 'Hey, buddy, turn your boy loose.' So, all in all, I would call the night a draw.

On one occasion, we took a wrong turning on leaving the club and became hopelessly lost on the vast Air Force base. Out of nowhere came two security vehicles and we were unceremoniously arrested at gunpoint – we had been heading for a restricted area and been picked up on radar. We were individually required to roughly sketch a layout of the club we had played – where the bar was in relation to the stage, toilets, etc. Finally convinced that we were merely poor struggling musicians, they courteously but firmly escorted us off the base.

And while we happily and profitably played the debs balls and Air Force bases, unbelievably there was no competition from the showband 'big boys', who were still playing the Irish venues. Oh! What might have been?

24. Opportunity Knocks for the Showbands

From 1956 to 1978, ITV Thames Television produced a hugely popular talent show, 'Opportunity Knocks', from its studios at Teddington Lock. The programme was presented by Hughie Green, one of the most famous faces on television at the time. An appearance on 'Opportunity Knocks' was the dream of every aspiring but unknown talent. Without doubt, it was the springboard to national and international stardom for many household names, such as Freddie Starr, Les Dawson, Frank Carson, Tom O'Connor, Paper Lace, Peters and Lee, Little and Large and Sue Pollard (later of 'Hi de Hi' fame, who was beaten on the night by a singing dog – honest!). The list goes on, although some stars, when they later became famous, were not prepared to acknowledge that they had ever appeared on the programme.

One of the show's strengths was the sheer diversity of the acts it featured. The variety was endless: pipe bands, belly dancers, barbershop quartets, comedians, pop groups, operatic societies, whistlers, steel bands, instrumentalists, vocalists and yes, showbands. The first step on the road to opportunity was a letter of application, after which, if you were very lucky, you were invited to a regional audition. In 1971 my band, New City Sounds,

KINGS

KINGS

KINGS

KINGS

KINGS

Ring a King at Naas - 7269
or Dublin - 974646

MANAGER. PAT M°GAAR, NAAS, CO. KILDARE.

The Kings, from Naas, were one of the showbands who made an appearance on 'Opportunity Knocks'.

got the 'call-up'. On arrival at the venue we were met by utter chaos – crowds of performers piled in together, children in tears, parents complaining loudly, disputes over who was first in line and how much space you could occupy. To get our equipment into the hall, we had to do battle with a steel band who were manhandling their gear out after an unsuccessful audition. No quarter was given.

Although everyone who had been called up had been given a specified appointment time, it mattered for nothing as the day's agenda fell hopelessly behind schedule. It suddenly made sense that the more experienced acts turned up at the crack of dawn. When an act's turn finally came, they were forced to set up in any space they could find around the hall, shoulder to shoulder with the next act. And every performance – the little time each act had to create the best impression – took place while competing acts were setting up, stripping down, tuning up and arguing about electric power points. It came down to holding your ground, brazening it out, putting a smile on and doing your business against all the odds.

I remember thinking that the audition itself was an anticlimax after all that, and also a pretty clinical affair, as Hughie Green and his team moved from act to act. Each 'spot' was strictly limited to three minutes, but sometimes an act was cut off in midstream with a firm, 'Thank you, who have we next?' – the equivalent, I guess, of, 'Don't call us; we'll call you.' If you got to

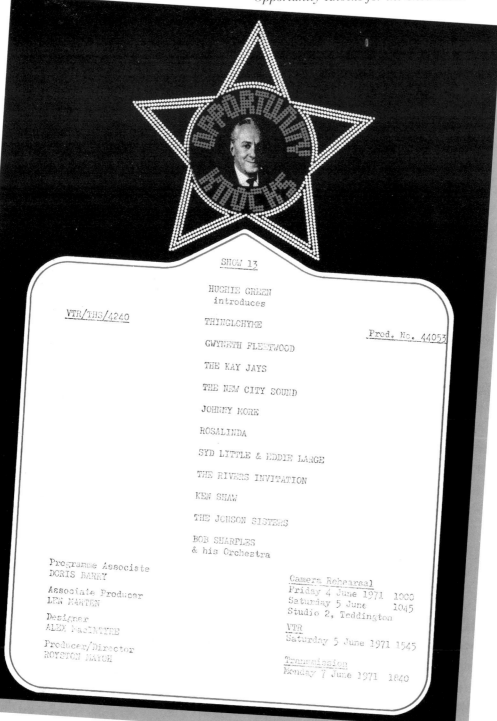

SHOW 13

VTR/THS/4240

HUGHIE GREEN
introduces

THINGLOHYME

Prod. No. 44053

GWYNETH FLEETWOOD

THE KAY JAYS

THE NEW CITY SOUND

JOHNNY MORE

ROSALINDA

SYD LITTLE & EDDIE LARGE

THE RIVERS INVITATION

KEN SHAW

THE JOHSON SISTERS

BOB SHARPLES
& his Orchestra

Programme Associate
DORIS BARRY

Associate Producer
LEN MARTEN

Designer
ALEX MacINTYRE

Producer/Director
ROYSTON MAYOH

Camera Rehearsal
Friday 4 June 1971   1000
Saturday 5 June   1045
Studio 2, Teddington

VTR
Saturday 5 June 1971 1545

Transmission
Monday 7 June 1971 1840

**My band, New City Sounds, were winners on Hughie Green's
'Opportunity Knocks' in 1971. Little and Large were among the other acts.**

finish your spot and were asked for a second number it was considered a green light; you were in with a fighting chance. We were thrilled when we were asked to do two further numbers, and our hopes were very high.

The long-awaited letter finally arrived, requiring us to attend Thames Television studios on the following Thursday, Friday and Saturday, 3-5th June 1971. Thursday and Friday were devoted to rehearsals – primarily for the camera crew and production team, as the acts were expected to have their three-minute spot polished by this stage. These two days also allowed Bob Sharples, the musical arranger, to complete his arrangements for any single singing act. Saturday morning saw a full dress rehearsal, at which Hughie Green made his first appearance. The man was a complete professional, and he slotted straight into his role with consummate ease. The show was pre-recorded on the Saturday afternoon and transmitted on Monday evening at 7pm. There were six acts on each show and, although there was a studio audience vote at the end of each show, the winners were actually chosen from a nationwide postal vote. The winners would then be recalled for an appearance on the next show. I can tell you that we didn't

Two great voices: Kelley of the Nevada showband (above) and Red Hurley (right). Opposite: the Victors showband from Cork, led by Art Supple.

stray very far from the telephone on the Wednesday morning after the show, hoping for another summons to London. And the call came. The viewers had cast their vote for us!

We won again the next week, and were recalled for a third appearance. At the end of each series, the winners were invited back to appear on the special 'All-Winners' show, so we made our fourth appearance then. This perform-ance was more relaxed and more of a party, as it was purely a showcase and there was no actual competition involved. I recall that Little and Large and Johnny More were on that particular show. There was a terrific atmosphere. In 1975 I had the privilege of returning to 'Opportunity Knocks' as leader of the Las Vegas showband.

In terms of our progress on the show, I'm convinced that the showband for-mat was the 'ace' in our pack. The standard showband combination of colour, movement, musical ability and neat appearance was the textbook formula for audition success on 'Opportunity Knocks'. Any decent showband had a dis-tinct advantage, as Tony Stevens, the Cotton Mill Boys, and the Kings show-band were to discover. It was a hugely enjoyable experience, and very rewarding, as success on the show opened up the bands to promoters and an influx of new bookings and venues

'Opportunity Knocks' went off the air in 1978. In 1987 the BBC tried to revive the show, but times had changed and the format had lost most of its appeal. However, it has to be acknowledged that in its time it made a tremendous contribution to the careers and futures of many of the best-known names in show business.

25. A Long, Long Way from Clare to Here

Being in a showband took lads from obscure villages in the middle of Ireland to places that they would have had difficulty locating on the revolving globe of their schoolroom days. One journey that especially stands out in my memory began in a little hall in Ennis, County Clare. It was the early 'sixties and I was standing in at a gig with the Ciaran Kelly Band. My colleague and lifelong friend Frankie McDonald, who later played with Joe Dolan and the Drifters, was on trumpet that night. At the time the 'Tijuana sound' – a unique close harmony trumpet sound created by Herb Alpert and his Tijuana Brass – was very popular and after playing a tune called 'Mexican Shuffle' I turned to Frankie and jokingly said, 'One day, we'll play that in Mexico.'

Over thirty years later, on 18 September 1997, Frankie, Joe Flynn and myself are on holiday with our wives in America. On our way from San Diego to Phoenix we take a detour and head, like so many outlaws before us, for the Mexican border. As we pass through the Mexican checkpoint we unpack our trumpets and right there at the border post, with the Mexican flag billowing above us, the Mexico sign behind us, and the border police coming out to listen, we play 'Mexican Shuffle', 'South of the Border' and a tune appropriately named 'Mexico', fulfilling the promise made so many years before and very far away.

Four miles ahead lay Tijuana. There is a Denny's restaurant in the main street, a focal point, with lots of tables and chairs outside. We repeated the performance there in the glorious Mexican sunshine, joined by Joe Flynn, another ex-Saint and known by all in music circles in the Irish midlands and beyond. Joe had somehow bought, borrowed or otherwise acquired a tambourine for the occasion, and all that was missing was his 'Jake the Peg' routine. Joe, if you ever read this, 'the cheque is in the post'. Great fun, wonderful company, a promise fulfilled and a memory forever.

Then it was on to Las Vegas.

A twelve-year-old Frankie McDonald shakes hands with the legendary trumpeter Eddie Calvert.

26. A Breed Apart: Showband Characters

*'I was 100 percent in favour of the promoter making a little money – but not **too** much.'*
Ben Dolan, the Drifters

Like any successful business, the Irish showband relied as much on the make-up and character of its band members as on their musical abilities. Although the big 'star' and frontline name was important, a band needed a core of reliable, dependable people who were musically competent, easy-going and agreeable and had a belief in what they were doing. It was important that members had a sense of humour, showed up on time and pulled their weight when it came to carrying, setting up and stripping down band gear or driving the wagon when required.

Of course, the showband scene had its fair share of characters: the eccentrics, the comedians, the wheeler-dealers, the ones who were always good for a laugh. I can tell you that in my time I came across all sorts of personalities and temperaments.

There was the drummer who was master of the quick getaway. He spent the last two numbers of every gig stripping down his kit. Cymbals, hi-hat and ancillary gear mysteriously vanished without any apparent loss in sound, tempo or beat and by the time the national anthem was played he was down to

Drummer and showman extraordinaire – Joe McCarthy of the Dixies.

a token snare drum and bass drum.

Then, of course, there was Joe Mac of the Dixies, who stands head and shoulders above everyone else in the 'unforgettable characters' category of the showband chronicle. The stories of his antics and the pranks he played are legion. For one particular Dixies standard he decided he had enough time between one drum beat and the next to pick up his sticks, leap off the stage, run to the end of the ballroom and tap his drumsticks against the far wall, before dashing back on stage to come in dead on cue with the next percussion beat. And it worked well – until the punters decided to have some fun. Then it became an obstacle race, as Joe would be shouldered, tripped or otherwise hindered on his frantic progress back to the bandstand.

A less successful showband member was the guitarist who consistently arrived at the venue when the band gear had been conveniently set up by his fellow band members. With minutes to spare before showtime, he simply plugged in his amplifier, stood at the back and played. Although I have to admit that he played superbly, his priorities were always how much he would get paid, when the next break was coming up and what time the gig would finish.

It was not the showband spirit and he didn't last long.

There were a lot of 'lovable rogues' in the business, and I particularly remember a Corkman called Derek Dixon who was at one time the lead singer with Maurice Mulcahy. One Sunday lunchtime, he came into a club where I happened to be playing and before long was on stage singing with us. The owner, Jimmy Bannon, was at the bar surrounded by his regulars and jokingly shouted up, 'Dixon, you're singing the same feckin' songs for the last ten years.' Quick as a flash, Derek stopped singing and said, 'Bannon, you're paying the same feckin' money for the last ten years.'

The Saints' Frank Somers was a wonderful organiser, without even being aware of it. For the five years I played with him we never saw our passports in the line of duty. He handled everything – booking flights, hotels, ferries, etc. – with never a hitch. He even arranged the pick-up times and ensured they were adhered to – you were subjected to a right old rollicking if you did not make the departure deadline. He also drove the wagon and was a very good drummer into the bargain. We needed someone like him to keep us wayward youngsters in line at the time, and the band ran very much the smoother for him.

You may remember the famous Hammond organ that caused us so much ttrouble with transportation – well, that was the particular 'baby' of our band-leader, Syd Shine. To get a better contact with the instrument, Syd would remove his left shoe when playing the organ on stage. The band member nearest him would gradually edge the shoe away to the next person, and so on, until it was passed down into the crowd, where it almost inevitably disappeared, having done the rounds of the hall. Syd must have been the only man in Ireland with twenty-two right shoes!

And that organ is still going strong. Syd was so attached to it that, after the showbands had come to a halt, he decided to bring the Hammond onto his boat on the

A Hammond B3 organ.

Shannon. As it wouldn't go down the hatch in one piece, it was cut in two and then reassembled below deck. This evidently didn't do any great damage to the instrument as, when I called in to see Syd recently, I was able to do a decent rendition of 'South of the Border' on the old keys.

Guitarists always seemed to me to be a breed apart. I remember playing with one who was very highly educated and entertained us greatly on the long journeys home from the gigs, but could not bring himself to play a note past the appointed finishing time. If told up front, he had no problem with a 2am or 3am finish, but if a gig was going really well and an organiser asked us to play an extra hour, the guitarist would literally break down in tears, howling, 'But I've programmed myself.' I never understood it.

Showband managers kept an eye on the pennies, but sometimes were a bit too frugal for some band members' liking. Stories abound of bands being fitted out with the cast-off suits from other outfits (with no tailoring or adjutments made). I heard of a case where the band were thrilled to be given new Beatle boots, cuban heels and all, but discovered that the canny manager had bought them one size too small for each person, so that the band would not be tempted to wear 'his' stage footwear in their off-duty hours.

At one point we introduced a band rule that the last person into the wagon after each gig drove home. We had a very dedicated guitarist at the time who had an obsession about replicating the exact sound from the record we were covering, and to his credit he generally succeeded. He was, however, a particularly sensitive individual, so when he found himself last to the wagon for the ninth time running after a gig in Sutton-on-Sea (he also liked the ladies), he completely flipped and threw the van keys into an adjoining field. We spent an unsuccessful hour in the dark

THE INDIANS ARE BACK ON THE "DANCE PATH" AGAIN AFTER THEIR WELL EARNED HOLIDAYS.

TO-NIGHT THEY'RE IN THE NATIONAL, DUBLIN
FRIDAY—FIESTA, LETTERKENNY
SATURDAY—THE GAP, OMAGH.
SUNDAY, 1st OCT.—GRANADA, GRANARD
TUESDAY 3rd—COUNTY HALL, MULLINGAR
WEDNESDAY 4th—CARNLOUGH.

Brave men! The Indians are still going strong. Among them is Eamon Keane, father of TV3's Lorraine Keane.

Left: A case of mistaken identity! The quick-thinking Rhythm Stars.
Below: Dave Carter.

vainly searching for them, before eventually 'hot-wiring' the wagon to get home.

The award for cuteness and quick thinking must go to Steven Tracey, band-leader of the Mighty Rhythm Stars from Ballintubber. On one occasion the band found themselves unable to fulfil a gig in Donegal, either through double-booking or illness. Steven Tracey gambled that Donegal was so far away that the band might not be known there, and solved the problem by sending the Hawaii showband – in his bandwagon – to pass themselves off as the Mighty Rhythm Stars. He was pleasantly surprised the following day to receive a telephone call from the dance committee, thanking him for a marvellous night and offering him several more bookings!

27. The Decline

All good things come to an end, and the showband era inevitably ran out of steam. The reasons for the decline are many and varied. As early as the end of 1966, flaws and cracks were beginning to become apparent. After ten hectic years, the business began looking tired. Bands were splitting or folding as key men were lured away by opportunistic managers to start new bands (which rarely achieved the standards of the bands they had just left) and cream off the lion's share of the takings. While the managers and the key men did handsomely in this new set-up, the other band members were now on a weekly wage, or were simply paid a fee per gig. Resentment kicked in. The initial impetus of a group of energetic, enthusiastic and dedicated friends who had started the band was gone, and full commitment was now questionable. There were constant personnel changes. They fulfilled the gigs – just. There was no holiday pay and ordinary band members could see no long-term future. Inevitably, standards began to decline. The battery was rapidly discharging and it was now downhill all the way.

I think that, in an odd way, the showbands were also victims of their own success. They gave too much, consistently. There was so much variety, talent and ability from band after band that it became accepted, commonplace and expected. The punters became blasé. Like a box of luxury chocolates – too

A sad sight. Many of the big ballrooms have become warehouses and business premises.

many and you become sated. However, the showbands had had ten wonderful and very lucrative years, from 1957 to 1967, probably longer than many other music phenomena.

The attitudes of ballroom owners was another factor in the decline. There was a lack of investment in the venues, so the majority remained charmless, cold and purely functional, the owners' overriding priority being floor space and capacity, with scant attention paid to facilities or comfort. Alcohol was also still not available in the ballrooms. The Irish economy had grown faster than anyone had predicted and exports had risen by fifty percent in the period from 1960 to 1966. Jobs and money had begun to flow into the country. Ireland had the lowest personal taxation rate in Europe, and Sean Lemass's vision of 'an economy significantly stable to enable all the Irish to live in their own country' was no longer a pipe dream.

People were becoming more affluent, expecting and willing to pay for higher standards. It was becoming more acceptable for ladies to drink, and they were now demanding more than four walls and lemonade. The new music lounges, with their soft lighting, comfortable seating and proper heating, became the preferred option for a night out. Cannily, many of the punters took advantage of the free coaches to the big out-of-town ballrooms, but once there went instead to the nearest music lounge, spent the evening there and were ferried home again at the expense of the ballroom owner, without ever entering his premises. Country and Irish-style bands, which did not need a brass section and could operate with a smaller line-up, were becoming the order of the day in these new venues.

Showbands continued playing the ballroom circuit for another few years, but to diminishing crowds. This was not good news for the promoters, who were also becoming increasingly disenchanted by the spiralling fees of the showbands and their own ever-decreasing percentages of the door take. They began to book lesser-known bands. The coaches gradually stopped running, midweek dancing ceased, profits plunged, ballrooms closed and bands folded. The showband gravy train was running out of track. The downward cycle continued. Plush, customised bandwagons became an endangered species in the 'seventies. The ballroom building boom was long over and even the perpetual showband smile was wearing thin. Aware of the decline in ballroom attendances and tired of the constant travelling, a large number of band members opted for local work and residencies in the new lounges. Grass and weeds began to encroach on the car parks of the big ballrooms, as the work moved to the hotels and lounges. Many talented showband musicians left their bands to branch out as duos or solo artists. The big brass showband sound was almost gone.

Arthur O'Shaughnessy, writing about the Irish in the mid-nineteenth century, said, 'We are the music makers.' This was certainly true of the showbands, who were the music makers for a whole generation of Irish people.

28. The 'Show' is Over

In this new millennium there are no showbands in the true sense of the word. There are some extremely talented and successful stars with a backing band, such as Daniel O'Donnell, Brendan Shine, Joe Dolan and Foster & Allen, but showbands they are not. In these acts, the star is the main attraction. They play a concert programme to a seated audience. By comparison to the exuberant and often spontaneous style of the showbands, it is somewhat clinical and sanitised. We could almost be reverting back to the 'pit' orchestras of the early 1900s, the band being there merely to back the act. I think this is a real pity. When there is so much talent up there on stage with the star, I believe that featuring them can only enhance the show, give the 'star' a breather, knit the unit closer and, in the end, make it a better and more enjoyable act for both the musician and the audience. Sadly, it rarely happens.

Despite all the sophistication, the hi-tech equipment, lighting and props, today's show is missing the raw enthusiasm, the hunger, the tight-knit combined talent of a unit with only one aim: to entertain. Gone is one of the most important ingredients – the live, warm input and feedback that flowed from the dancing audience back to the bandstand. There was a feeling of being part of the show in the banter between audience and band members. The whole audience felt completely involved, not just the static, seated first eight rows. Gone also is the variety the original showbands had to offer – the different singers, the vast range of styles and the huge repertoire of country and western, pop, ballad, Irish, rock 'n' roll and skiffle songs, along with the special numbers like the monologues, or those punchy brass arrangements of 'William Tell', 'Brass Band Samba', 'Mexico', and so on.

As far as the showband is concerned, 'the song is ended ...' but for all of us who were involved, 'the melody lingers on ...' and on ... and on.

DERRICK OF THE SOUNDS

Right: 'The Doc' and 'El Tel'. Terry Wogan plays support to Doc Carroll.

29. The Legacy

'Having been fortunate enough to play with most of the showband icons, albeit forty years later, we have nothing but respect and admiration for their talent and showmanship, more especially as they did it all without the help of today's modern sound technology and digital enhancements.'
Keith and Loraine, The Showband Show'

Music today, both in Ireland and further afield, benefits enormously from the influence of the showbands. Currently there are at least half-a-dozen local radio shows devoted solely to the showband era. Why, after forty odd years, is the music still so popular? Who are these listeners? What is the attraction? The Saturday morning 'Showband Show' on Shannonside/Northern Sound Radio has been running for five years and has gone from strength to strength. When RTÉ's 'Nationwide' programme screened a recent Brendan Bowyer performance from Waterford's Jury's hotel, it attracted a viewership in excess of half a million people. The regular 'Showband Show Hucklebuck Tour', which features Brendan Bowyer, Eileen Reed and Brendan O'Brien, sells out all forty-two show in every corner of Ireland.

In Northern Ireland, BBC radio and television personality George Jones devised and presented a showband tribute show, 'Do You Come Here Often?', which packed them in at the opening of Belfast's Waterfront Hall. The reaction to the show was so phenomenal that it has been revived on numerous

Derrick and the Sounds.

occasions, not only at the Waterfront, but also at Derry's Rialto entertainment centre. Performers on the show have included Brian Coll, the Witnesses, Eileen Reed, Tina, Brendan Bowyer, Larry Cunningham, the Melody Aces, Dave Glover, Sean Fagan and Sean Dunphy, who proved that their popularity remained as undiminished as ever. On each outing, the show has been fully booked out even before the final line-up has been announced; on its last run, it filled the Waterfront for eight consecutive nights. George Jones is himself a veteran of several showbands, starting with the Monarchs – whose line-up also included Van Morrison – then the Silhouettes and later one of the country's top bands, the Dave Glover Band.

Showband veterans have brought the best aspects of their craft to their new ventures down through the years. They have promoted the showband values, discipline and traditions by example in whatever genres of music they have found themselves. You can still see it today in their easy-going, professional style, their presentation and their belief in putting the punter first, last and always. Performers such as Paddy Cole, Sonny Knowles, Joe Dolan and Dickie Rock display a consummate ease that makes it all seem effortless but comes from years of dedication and pure professionalism.

One spin-off of the showband era and a testimony to its continuing popularity is the great success of Athlone's Showband Show, a showband that plays a programme replicating the 'sixties showband style and sound. Every year they tour the country, backing one of the major showband stars. They play to packed venues and

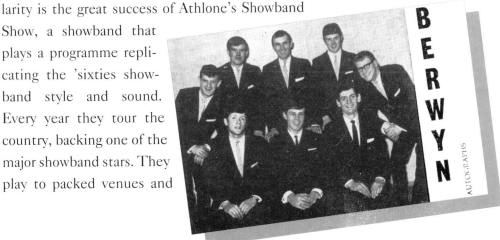

receive rave notices in what is a true and faithfully-produced tribute to the original showbands. They have done their homework diligently and present a scintillating, punchy and attention-grabbing show that any of the top original showband icons would have been proud to be associated with. It is all there – the stage dress, the line-up, the programme selection, the projection, the 'steps', the sound, the enthusiasm and the talent – and all of this comes from a band whose members weren't even born when the showband was king.

It is no coincidence that Loraine, Keith and drummer Peter of the Showband Show happen to be the offspring of my old friend, Frankie McDonald, Saint and Joe Dolan bandmember . Their mother, Mia, is also a musician, who spent some years playing keyboard on the nation's bandstands. It is good to report that the showband genes are so strong and healthy.

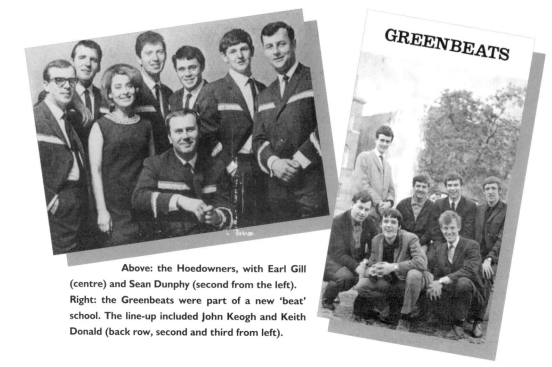

Above: the Hoedowners, with Earl Gill (centre) and Sean Dunphy (second from the left). Right: the Greenbeats were part of a new 'beat' school. The line-up included John Keogh and Keith Donald (back row, second and third from left).

30. A Deserved Tribute

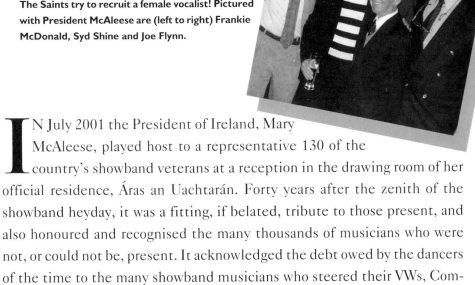

The Saints try to recruit a female vocalist! Pictured with President McAleese are (left to right) Frankie McDonald, Syd Shine and Joe Flynn.

IN July 2001 the President of Ireland, Mary McAleese, played host to a representative 130 of the country's showband veterans at a reception in the drawing room of her official residence, Áras an Uachtarán. Forty years after the zenith of the showband heyday, it was a fitting, if belated, tribute to those present, and also honoured and recognised the many thousands of musicians who were not, or could not be, present. It acknowledged the debt owed by the dancers of the time to the many showband musicians who steered their VWs, Commers or luxury bandwagons down pot-holed country roads on frosty or balmy nights, to bring music and entertainment to every dancehall and ballroom in the country.

The gathering included not only the musicians but also some of the band managers, the movers and fixers of the business at the time. The party was buzzing as many musicians, friends and colleagues were reunited and old stories recollected and retold with, I am sure, improvements and embellishments acquired in the retelling and passing of the years.

Among the guests was my friend Frankie McDonald, trumpeter with Joe Dolan for thirty years and someone who could be said to have served his apprenticeship in the business. It was Frankie's second visit to Áras an Uachtarán; the first time was during the visit of President John Fitzgerald Kennedy to Ireland in 1963, under very different circumstances. On that occasion Frankie was outside looking in – a young army bandsman, who played on the lawn for the entertainment of the visiting dignitaries. I know this to be true, because I was the one sitting next to him!

Although I could not get to the 2001 event, three of my ex-band members were in attendance, and later delighted in quoting me chapter and verse on the whole proceedings. One was the eighty-two-years-young Syd Shine, my first bandleader with the Saints. Johnny Quigley from Derry – yes, that Johnny Quigley – reminded Syd of the many times his band had visited the city. On these occasions both bands would amalgamate after the dancers had left, orchestrations would be handed out and they would play for a further two hours together. No overtime payment was involved, just sheer enjoyment. It reflected the mindset and attitude of showband musicians then, and of the period in general. Sometimes there would be twenty-three musicians in total on stage and not a minidisc in sight.

The President quoted Seamus Heaney on the Ireland of his parents' day, about how the people were 'living under high-banked clouds of resignation'. That, she said, was what the showbands changed – they blew those clouds away. 'While the showband world has changed,' she went on, 'and the entertainment world has moved on, we owe all you people a debt and this reception is by way of saying we have not forgotten.'

Quoting Fr Brian Darcy, the showbiz priest, who was also present, she said that in the days of the showband, 'ecstasy did not come in tablet form – it was rather a perspiration-drenched night at a country crossroads under the canvas of a five-pole marquee, dancing to the unique sound of an Irish showband.' Recalling the Miami showband massacre in 1975, she said, 'The dark shadows which gathered after that tragic night were in such sharp contrast to the gaiety of the showband scene, a place where young people met, where romances flourished, where even the best efforts of the parish priest to impose space for the Holy Ghost between dancing couples could not dampen the sense of fun and liberation.'

As the veterans chatted and reminisced, one thing was evident: just like those evenings on the bandstands long ago, the smiles were many and as always they were broad and they were free.

Epilogue

'Socially and musically, the showbands played a huge part in the development of the Ireland of the '60s. Sometimes, some people find it too easy to "air-brush" out the showbands' contribution'.
Ronan Collins, RTÉ

It has become fashionable in some quarters today to slate the showbands, to dismiss their contribution to Irish life and rubbish their music. While everyone is entitled to an opinion, it is nevertheless sad that most of this criticism comes from fellow musicians, significantly, of another generation. What they are saying is, in my view, not just ill-advised, immature and unjust, but also incorrect. It does nothing for the stature of those critics or of the music profession as a whole. Trying to impose twenty-first-century tastes and values on the music of a different era is a pointless exercise. The impact of the showbands has to be gauged from the perspective of the period from the late 'fifties to the late 'sixties, with its particular social and cultural attitudes and its very different economic situation. The views of those rock stars who actually played in a showband are totally different, and their respect is obvious.

In an interview with Niall Stokes of *Hot Press* magazine in March 2000, Van 'The Man' Morrison spoke of his showband roots with the Monarchs: 'Showbands were probably the only entity in Ireland that were getting work – I mean I don't know anyone that wasn't in a showband. Some of these bands had a very high calibre of musicianship so it was something they could have

My old army band colleague, Noel Melia (third from left) played with the Ravens.

done in Las Vegas, it was actually a show. You know, they did everything, they did comedy, right, they did top ten, they did jazz, they did impersonations – you know, it was a very professional show. It wasn't just a matter of guys doing steps and wearing suits.'

The late, great Rory Gallagher certainly had no regrets about his time with the Fontana Showband. 'I had tried to get a group together at school in Cork, it only lasted one night,' he recalled. 'I was still doing the odd show on my own – talent shows and charity shows, Pioneer rallies. So when I saw an add in a paper – "Showband needs guitar player" – I said, well I'll give it a bash. These fellows were doing two or three gigs a week and I could plug into an AC30 – the amplifier I had at home was only a four-watt Selmer! I handled the rock 'n' roll department, basically. The two years I had with them was fun – at the age of sixteen.'

Sure, there were poor showbands, just as there are poor groups today. But ask the people who really matter – the punters of that time, who travelled miles, packed the ballrooms and experienced at first hand the excitement, entertainment and sparkle of the boys in the mohair and shiny suits. I know what their answer was then, and I would bet that answer is the same today. Ultimately, as customers, theirs is the only opinion that really matters.

As I drive around Ireland today I see those self-same ballrooms, now sadly relegated for use as store rooms and furniture stores, but still capable of rekindling so many memories. I think of all the dreams they triggered long ago – not just for the bands, but also for the dancers; the romances that began in them; the weddings that followed and the families that blossomed from those weddings. The brass may now be muted, the rhythm sections hushed and the drums silent, but the echoes still reverberate for all of us fifty-somethings.

We, at least, will always remember with pride that we were part of the show-band generation. We were fortunate to enjoy the professionalism, presence, grace and the sheer entertaining talents of some super showmen. They brought enjoyment, excitement and inspiration to hundreds of thousands and helped change the social fabric of a whole country. They may be gone but they leave an indelible footprint.

With the lights dimmed, the ballroom doors shut and bolted and the music ended, it only remains to say just once more, as we did so many times, in so many venues, so long ago: 'Good night, God Bless and Safe Home.'

Appendix 1

Some Irish Showbands of the 1960s

The Airchords Showband	Dublin	The Bluebeats Showband	Dublin
The Action Showband	Dublin	The Blue Diamonds	Dublin
The Alpine Seven	Meath	The Blue Zodiacs	Dublin
The Ray Allen Orchestra	Dublin	The Blazers Showband	Galway
The Altonaires Showband	Dublin	The Black Aces Showband	Kilkenny
The Alley Katz	Lambeg	The Blue Rockets Showband	Cork
The Ambassadors Orchestra	Belfast	The Jimmy Boyce Showband	Belfast
The Amigoes Showband	Belfast	The Chris Byrne Showband	Dublin
The Angels Showband	Dublin	The Pat Bourke Seven	Tipperary
The Apollo Showband	Holywood	The Bromwells Showband	Cork
The Arabs Showband	Belfast	The Bridesiders Showband	Waterford
The Aran Showband	Dublin	The Jack Brierly Showband	Belfast
The Arcadians Showband	Meath	The Brothers Showband	Newtownabbey
The Archers Showband	Cork	The Brunswick Showband	Belfast
The Arrivals Showband	Cork	The Cadets Showband	Dublin
The Atlantis Showband	Dublin	The Johnny Calvert Showband	Belfast
The Atlantic Showband	Waterford	The Capri Four	Cork
The Jim Bacon Orchestra	Dublin	The Gene Carr Showband	Cork
The Toby Bannon Orchestra	Dublin	The Capitol Showband	Dublin
The Bandits Showband	Tuam	The Carousel Showband	Dublin
The Banshees	Belfast	The Cavalier Showband	Whitehead
The Barnstormers	Dublin	The Central Seven Showband	Ferbane
The Barons Showband	Dublin	The Tony Chambers Showband	Mayo
The Barristers Showband	Derry	The Checkmates	Belfast
The Syd Bates Orchestra	Belfast	The Chessmen	Dublin
The Bats Showband	Belfast	The City Trio	Derry
The Beavers Showband	Bray	The Citizens Showband	Dublin
The Beat Minstrels	Louisburgh	The Classics Showband	Mullingar
The Belaires Showband	Ballyclare	The Clubmen	Dublin
The Beltona Showband	Bushmills	The Bud Clancy Showband	Limerick
The Berwyn Showband	Dublin	The Clavichords	Dublin
The Bluebeats Showband	Belfast	The Claxton Showband	Drumquin

The Cliffords Showband	Dublin	The Derry City Showband	Derry
The Clipper Carlton Showband	Strabane	The Derrytones Showband	Derry
The Columbia Showband	Wicklow	The Dixies Showband	Cork
The Comets Showband	Omagh	The Alex Dixon Band	Newtownabbey
The Commodores Showband	Dublin	The Dave Dixon Showband	Clones
The Donie Collins Showband	Limerick	The Jim Doherty Trio	Dublin
The College Showband	Limerick	The Domino Showband	Cork
The Conquerors	Galway	The Donnays Showband	Belfast
The College Boys	Belfast	The Drumbeat Showband	Lifford
The Collegemen Showband	Dublin	The Jimmy Dunny Showband	Newbridge
The Noel Connell Showband	Dundonald	The Dynamics Showband	Dublin
The Joe Coughlan orchestra	Dublin	The Drifters Showband	Mullingar
The Coral Showband	Ballymena	The Easybeats	Ballina
The Cordettes Showband	Loughrea	The Echoes	Arklow
The Corsairs Showband	Belfast	The Embassy Showband	Derry
The Pascal Cosgrove Showband	Foxford	The Emperors Showband	Derry
The Cossacks Showband	Ballymena	The Empire Showband	Limerick
The Countrymen Showband	Clara	The Encores Showband	Belfast
The Courtelles Showband	Belfast	The Ennjay Quartet	Belfast
The Cortina Showband	Nenagh	The Everglades Showband	Dublin
The Crackaways Showband	Clara	The Esquire Allstars	Derry
The Crescendos Showband	Belfast	The Exiles Showband	Belfast
The Creole Showband	Athlone	The Fab Five	Mayo
The Creatures Showband	Dublin	The Falcons Showband	Bangor
The Bob Cupples Showband	Belfast	The Jim Farley Showband	Dublin
The Cyclones Showband	Belfast	The Federals Showband	Belfast
The Cyclones Showband	Dublin	The John Fitzgerald Archestra	Dublin
The Michael Dalton Showband	Cork	The Fernandos	Roscommon
The Danstimers Showband	Belfast	The Finnavons	Monaghan
The Davitt Brothers Showband	Ferns	The Firehouse Five & Two	Westmeath
The Dee-Jay Dance Band	Strabane	The Five Silhouettes	Cork
The Mick Delahunty Orchestra	Clonmel	The Jack Flahive Orchestra	Dublin
The Delta Allstars	Derry	The Flamingoes	Dundalk
The Delta Boys Showband	Drogheda	The Florida Showband	Derry
The Demons Showband	Lurgan	The Johnny Flynn Showband	Tuam
The Deputies Showband	Belfast	The Pat Friel Showband	Westport
The Derek Joys	Waterford	The Fontana Showband	Cork

The Freshmen Showband	Ballymena	The Pat Irwin Allstars	Cork
The Johnny Gavin Showband	Dublin	The Jivenaires Showband	Boyle
The Gaylords Showband	Lisburn	The Jimmy Johnston Showband	Lisburn
The Gearytones Showband	Cork	Joe Judge & The Jury	Belfast
Gene & The Gents	Enniskillen	The Jokers Showband	Derry
The Giants Showband	Dublin	The George Jordan Showband	Ballina
The Earl Gill Showband	Dublin	The Kamels Showband	Dublin
The Globetrotters Showband	Armagh	The Keynotes Showband	Donegal
The Dave Glover Showband	Newtownabbey	The Kentones Showband	Kilkenny
The Graduates Showband	Meath	The Kestrels Showband	Cork
The Grafton Showband	Cookstown	The Neil Kearns Showband	Dublin
The Grenada Showband	Dublin	The Keymen Showband	Dublin
The Granada Showband	Dungannon	The Kerry Blues	Kerry
The Gravediggers Showband	Belfast	The Kings Showband	Naas
The Greenbeats	Dublin	The Kingston Showband	Derry
The Grenadiers Showband	Belfast	The Lamplighters Showband	Dublin
The Jack Glynn Quintet	Limerick	The Las Vegas Showband	Dublin
The Golden Aces Showband	Ballinrobe	The Leaders Showband	Westport
The Golden Seven	Lifford	The Walter Lewis Showband	Ballymena
The Great 8	Holywood	The Maurice Lynch Showband	Castleblaney
The Jack Hanley Showband	Templemore	The Madlads Showband	Belfast
The Harlequins Showband	Belfast	The Madison Showband	Mullingar
The Fred Hanna Danceband	Newtownabbey	The Magnificent 7 Showband	Derry
The Harmony Aces Showband	Tassagh	The Majestic Showband	Tralee
The Jack Harrison Showband	Belfast	The Manhattan Showband	Dublin
The Hilton Showband	Warrenpoint	The Manhatten Showband	Belfast
The Hoedowners	Dublin	The Marines Showband	Letterkenny
The Huntsmen Showband	Maze	The MarkV Showband	Omagh
The Hurricanes Showband	Dundalk	The Martells Showband	Belfast
The Hustlers Showband	Dublin	The Masters Showband	Derry
The Impact Showband	Cork	The Gay McIntyre Showband	Derry
The Indians	Dublin	The Matadors Showband	Belfast
The Inmates Showband	Dublin	The Melody Aces	Omagh
The International Showband	Derry	The Mellowchords Showband	Emyvale
The Interns Showband	Portrush	The Mellowtone Showband	Belfast
The Innkeepers Showband	Belfast	The Memphis Showband	Dublin
The Invaders Showband	Ballycastle	The Mexicans Showband	Bray

The Merry Minstrels Showband	Delvin	The Olympia Showband	Galway
The M.I.Five Showband	Belfast	The Olympic Showband	Cork
The Mighty Avons	Ballyhoise	The Omega Showband	Limerick
The Mighty Rhythm Aces	Donegal	The Orients Showband	Belfast
The Mighty Rhythm Boys	Buncrana	The Oriole Showband	Shrule
The Mighty Rhythm Stars	Ballintubber	The Orlando Showband	Ballymoney
The Miami Showband	Dublin	The Orpheus Showband	Belfast
The Millionaires Showband	Dublin	The Pacific Showband	Dublin
The Misfits Showband	Belfast	The Panama Showband	Dublin
The John Mitchell Showband	Ballymena	The Paragon Seven	Dublin
The Monaco Showband	Dublin	The Frank Parkes Showband	Dublin
The Moonglows Showband	Dublin	The Pavillionaires Showband	Dublin
The Mounties Showband	Dublin	The Pendulums Showband	Newtownabbey
The Monarchs Showband	Belfast	The Phantoms Showband	Dunmurray
The Monarchs Showband	Limerick	The Pioneers Showband	Gilford
The Montana Showband	Kilkenny	The Platters/Plattermen Showband	Omagh
The Modernaires Showband	Cork	The Playmates Showband	Tralee
The James Morrow Band	Belfast	The Tommy Power Showband	Cork
The Humphrey Murphy Showband	Dublin	The Premier Aces Showband	Ballintubber
The Paddy McCafferty Showband	Ballybofey	The Presidents Showband	Omagh
The Johnny McMahon Showband	Limerick	The Prophets Showband	Belfast
The Alex McKee Band	Belfast	The Pyramids Showband	Athlone
The Tom McKechnie Band	Belfast	The Radiant Showband	Scartaglin
The Maurice Mulcahy Orchestra	Mitchelstown	The Ravens Showband	Dublin
The Musicmakers Showband	Cork	The Ramblers Showband	Elphin
The Mystery Men Showband	Dublin	The Real McCoy	Dublin
The Mystics Showband	Belfast	The Red Admirals Showband	Ballymena
The Nashville Showband	Dublin	The Regal Showband	Cork
The Nevada Showband	Derry	The Regency Showband	Belfast
The Nevada Showband	Dublin	The Rio Showband	Lifford
The George Newman Band	Belfast	The Rollin Tones	Dublin
The New Yorkers Showband	Dublin	The Royal Aces	Dungarvan
The Nomads Showband	Kilkenny	The Royal Blues	Claremorris
The Dermot O'Brien Showband	Dublin	The Royal Stars Showband	Drogheda
The Tommy O'Brien Orchestra	Dublin	The Royal Showband	Waterford
The Michael O'Callaghan Showband	Buttevant	The Royaltones	Ballinderry
The Oceans Showband	Belfast	The Royal Viceroys	Drogheda

The Jack Ruane Showband	Ballina	The Sylvians Showband	Belfast
The Rhythmaires Showband	Ballymoney	The Tahiti Showband	Derry
The Saints Showband	Athlone	The Teenbeats Showband	Dublin
The Santa Fe Showband	Strabane	The Teenbeats Showband	Newtownabbey
The Savoy Showband	Waterford	The Telstars Showband	Tralee
The Savoy Swing Seven	Carrick on Shannon	Them	Belfast
The Scarlet Seven	Crossmolina	The Thunderbeats Showband	Cork
The Seekers Showband	Belfast	The Tonics Showband	Bray
The Senators Showband	Belfast	The Topflights Showband	Ballina
The Serenaders Showband	Belturbet	The Topical Showband	Carlow
The Sierra Showband	Dublin	The Toppers Showband	Drogheda
The Silver Dollars	Armagh	The Toreadors Showband	Cork
The Sinners Showband	Longford	The Tremors Showband	Belfast
The Slick-Six Showband	Tipperary	The Ukons Showband	Kilkenny
The Chick Smith Showband	Dublin	The U.S.A. Showband	Dublin
The Snowdrifters Showband	Cookstown	The Vaqueres Showband	Belfast
The Somertones Showband	Cork	The Velvetones Showband	Belfast
The Sonics Showband	Belfast	The Viceroy Showband	Cork
The Sounds Showband	Fintona	The Victors Showband	Cork
The Soundtracks Showband	Belfast	The Viva Showband	Lurgan
The Spectres Showband	Belfast	The Vibratones	Belfast
The Swallows Showband	Dublin	The Brose Walsh Showband	Castlebar
The Skyliners Showband	Cork	The Washington Showband	Belfast
The Skymasters Showband	Strabane	The Billy White Band	Belfast
The Skyrockets Showband	Enniskillen	The Bob Wilson Showband	Belfast
The Starliners Showband	Belfast	The Jack Wilson Showband	Belfast
The Strands Showband	Belfast	The Witnesses Showband	Belfast
The Stratatones Showband	Belfast	The Kevin Woods Showband	Drumshanbo
The Strollers Showband	Belfast	The Woodchoppers Showband	Derry
The Students Showband	Antrim	The Woodpeckers Showband	Dundalk
The Swingbeats Showband	Cork	The Young Clavons	Dublin
The Swinging Safari Showband	Monaghan	The Young Shadows	Dublin
The Swingtime Aces Showband	Athenry	The Young Vikings	Dundalk
The Swinging Vicounts Showband	Donegal	The Zodiacs Showband	Keady

Appendix 2

Some Irish Ballrooms of the 1960s

Antrim

Carrera Ballroom	Ballyclare
Floral Hall Ballroom	Newtownabbey
Flamingo Ballroom	Ballymena
Kings Arms Ballroom	Larne
Richview Ballroom	Islandmagee
Pond Park Ballroom	Lisburn
Plaza Ballroom	Larne
Top Hat Ballroom	Larne
Top Hat Ballroom	Lisburn
Quay Road Hall	Ballycastle
Armagh Ballroom	Moira
Calypso Ballroom	Lurgan
Savoy Ballroom	Portadown
Tempo Ballroom	Moira

Belfast

Astor Ballroom	College Court Boom Boom Room
Gala Ballroom	Arthur Square
Gala Ballroom	Victoria Street
Fiesta Ballroom	Hamilton Street
Sammy Houston's	Great Victoria St
Maxim's Ballroom	Fountain Street
Orchid Ballroom	King Street
Romano's Ballroom	Queen Street
Plaza Ballroom	Chichester Street
Orpheus Ballroom	York Street

Carlow

Crofton Hotel	Carlow
Ritz Ballroom	Carlow
Royal Hotel Ballroom	Carlow

Cavan

Granada Ballroom	Kingscourt
Lough Ramor Farmers	Virginia
Wonderland Ballroom	Cavan
Star Ballroom	Ballyconnell
Sports Centre Ballroom	Kinnypottle
Ritz Ballroom	Killeshandra

Clare

Kincora Ballroom	Kilaloe
Hydro Hotel Ballroom	Kilkee
New Hall Ballroom	Ennis
Arch Ballroom	Sixmilebridge
Royal Spa Hotel Ballroom	Lisdoonvarna

Cork

Arcadia Ballroom	Lr Glanmire Road
Caroline Ballroom	Drimoleague
Gaiety Ballroom	Military Road
Hiland Ballroom	Newmarket
Metropole Hotel Ballroom	Mac Curtain St
Imperial Hotel Ballroom	South Mall
Palm Court Ballroom	Caroline Street
Stardust Ballroom	Cork
Lilac Ballroom	Enniskeane
Majestic Ballroom	Mallow
Maple Ballroom	Millstreet
Mayflower Ballroom	Mitchelstown
Cronin's Hotel Ballroom	Charleville
Majorca Ballroom	Crosshaven
Redbarn Ballroom	Youghal
Showboat Ballroom	Youghal

Star Ballroom	Millstreet
State Hall	Midleton
Top Hat Ballroom	Fermoy

Donegal

Astoria Ballroom	Bundoran
Abbey Ballroom	Ballyshannon
Borderland Ballroom	Muff
Butt Hall	Ballybofey
Fiesta Ballroom	Letterkenny
Country Club Ballroom	Termon
Mulroy Ballroom	Kerrykeel
North Star Ballroom	Letterkenny
Pavesi Ballroom	Donegal
Rockhill Castle	Kerrykeel
Orchid Ballroom	Lifford
Sea View Hotel Ballroom	Bunbeg
Foresters Ballroom	Killybegs
Atlantic Ballroom	Clonmany
Malin Hotel Ballroom	Malin
Hotel Ballroom	Raphoe

Down

Ashleigh Ballroom	Millisle
Caproni's Ballroom	Bangor
Castle Ballroom	Banbridge
Central Ballroom	Banbridge
Central Ballroom	Newcastle
Locarno Ballroom	Portaferry
Moat Ballroom	Donaghadee
Royal Arms Ballroom	Omagh
Osbourne Ballroom	Warrenpoint
Queen's Hall Ballroom	Newtownards
Royal Ballroom	Dundonald

Dublin City

| Four Provinces (TV Club) | Harcourt St |

Crystal Ballroom	Anne Street
Olympic Ballroom	Pleasants Street
Metropole Ballroom	O'Connell St
Clery's Ballroom	O'Connell St
National Ballroom	Parnell Square
Kingsway Ballroom	Dorset Street
Barry's Hotel Ballroom	Denmark Street
Town & Country Ballroom	Parnell Square
Ierne Ballroom	Parnell Square
The Irish Club	Parnell Square
Adelaide Ballroom	Adelaide Road
Gresham Hotel	O'Connell St
Shelbourne Hotel	St Stephen's Grn
Intercontinental Hotel	Ballsbridge
Montrose Hotel	Stillorgan
St Francis Xavier Hall	Dublin

Dublin County

Top Hat Ballroom	Dun Laoghaire
Palm Beach Ballroom	Portmarnock
Country Club	Portmarnock
Palladium Ballroom	Rush
Pavilion Ballroom	Skerries
Grand Hotel Ballroom	Malahide
Spanish Arch Ballroom	Malahide
Rolestown Ballroom	Swords

Fermanagh

| Silver Sandal | Enniskillen |

Galway

Casino Ballroom	Castlerea
Las Vegas	Tuam
Seapoint Ballroom	Salthill
Hanger Ballroom	Salthill
Ocean Wave Hotel	Salthill
Classic Ballroom	Gort

Waldorf Ballroom	Woodford	**Laois**	
New Castle Ballroom	Dunmore	Danceland Ballroom	Portlaoise
Eagle Ballroom	Galway	Castle Ballroom	Mountrath
Esker Ballroom	Glenamaddy	Rockland Ballroom	Borris in Ossory
Emerald Ballroom	Ballinasloe	CYMS Ballroom	Portarlington
Top of the Town	Galway	Savoy Ballroom	Kilcormac

Kerry

		Leitrim	
Silver Slipper Ballroom	Kenmare	Rainbow Ballroom	Glenfarne
Brandon Ballroom	Tralee	McGowan's Ballroom	Kiltyclogher
Central Ballroom	Ballybunion	Mayflower Ballroom	Drumshanbo
CYMS	Killorglin	Doherty's Ballroom	Drumshanbo
Horan's Ballroom	Ballybunion		
Gala Ballroom	Killarney	**Limerick**	
Wavecrest Ballroom	Waterville	Jetland Ballroom	Caherdavin
Gleneagle Ballroom	Killarney	Olympic Ballroom	Newcastlewest
Las Vegas Ballroom	Listowel	Desmond Ballroom	Newcastlewest
Iveragh Ballroom	Cahirciveen	Cruise's Hotel	Limerick
John Marcus O'Sullivan	Firies	Flamingo	Abbeyfeale
Oisin Ballroom	Killorglin	Royal George Hotel	Limerick
White Sands Hotel	Ballyheigue	Morning Star	Bruff
Palace Ballroom	Annascaul	Oyster Ballroom	Dromkeen
St John's Hall	Tralee	Star Ballroom	Cappamore
		Stella Ballroom	Limerick
		Town Hall	Croom
Kildare		Glenside Ballroom	Glenmeedy
Lawlor's Ballroom	Naas		
Ideal Ballroom	Prosperous		
Town Hall Ballroom	Newbridge	**Longford**	
CYMS Ballroom	Kildare	Granada Ballroom	Granard
Town Hall Ballroom	Edenderry	Longford Arms Hotel	Longford
Dreamland Ballroom	Athy	Mostrim Arms Hotel	Edgeworthstown
		Town Hall Ballroom	Granard

Kilkenny			
Mayfair Ballroom	Kilkenny	**Louth**	
Friary Hall Ballroom	Kilkenny	Abbey Ballroom	Drogheda
CYMS Ballroom	Castlecomer	Adelphi Ballroom	Dundalk
Carlton Ballroom	Kilkenny	Derryhale Hotel	Dundalk

Castle Ballroom	Castlebellingham	Shamrock Ballroom	Binghamstown
Ardee Ballroom	Ardee	Shamrock Ballroom	Belmullet
Pavilion Ballroom	Blackrock	Starland Ballroom	Ballyhaunis
		Starlight Ballroom	Westport

Derry

		Ballycastle Ballroom	Ballycastle
Cameo Ballroom	Derry		
Castle Ballroom	Dungiven	**Meath**	
Corinthian Ballroom	Derry	Beechmount Ballroom	Navan
Embassy Ballroom	Derry	Headfort Arms Hotel	Kells
Golden Slipper Ballroom	Derry	Kilmoon Ballroom	Kilmoon
Silver Slipper Ballroom	Milligan	Eldorado Ballroom	Oldcastle
Limavady Agricultural Ballroom	Limavady	Royal Ballroom	Athboy
Mulroy Ballroom	Kerrykell	Russell Arms Hotel	Navan
Pallidrome Ballroom	Strabane	Town Hall Ballroom	Trim
Strand Ballroom	Portstewart	New Hall Ballroom	Slane
		Oasis Ballroom	Dunboyne

Mayo

		Monaghan	
Arcadia Ballroom	Belcarra		
Belclare House Hotel	Westport	Embassy Ballroom	Castleblaney
Belmullet Ballroom	Belmullet	Western Ballroom	Monaghan
Binghamstown Ballroom	Binghamstown	New Hall Ballroom	Emyvale
Corbett's Ballroom	Headford	Oasis Ballroom	Carrickmacross
Eclipse Ballroom	Ballyhaunis		
Gaiety Ballroom	Westport	**Offaly**	
Glenamoy Ballroom	Glenamoy	Kennedy's Ballroom	Banagher
Golden Olive Ballroom	Cong	Marian Hall Ballroom	Birr
Grove Ballroom	Ballina	Star Ballroom	Clara
Kilmeena Hall	Kilmeena	Central Ballroom	Tullamore
Maple Ballroom	Ballinrobe		
Moyland Ballroom	Ballina	**Roscommon**	
Mulranny Ballroom	Mulranny	Cloudland Ballroom	Rooskey
Pavilion Ballroom	Westport	Fairyland Ballroom	Roscommon
Pontoon Ballroom	Foxford	Tower Ballroom	Tarmonbarry
Royal Ballroom	Castlebar	Magnet Ballroom	Strokestown
Pavilion Ballroom	Westport	Elphin Social Centre	Elphin
Diamond Ballroom	Kiltimagh	Excell Ballroom	Ballymote
Savoy Ballroom	Claremorris		

Sligo

Silver Slipper Ballroom	Strandhill
Marine Ballroom	Enniscrone
Seafield Ballroom	Easkey
Finnerty's Ballroom	Rathlee
Culleen Ballroom	Culleen

Tipperary

Arcadia Ballroom	Cahir
County Ballroom	Cashel
Collin's Ballroom	Clonmel
Las Vegas Ballroom	Templemore
Minella Hotel	Clonmel
Ormonde Hotel	Nenagh
Oval Ballroom	Emly
Premier Ballroom	Thurles
Tower Ballroom	Tipperary

Tyrone

Melvin Ballroom	Irvinstown
Pallidrome Ballroom	Strabane
Star Ballroom	Omagh

Waterford

Olympia Ballroom	Waterford
Crystal Ballroom	Waterford
Haven Hotel	Dunmore East
Atlantic Ballroom	Tramore
Rainbow Ballroom	Kilmacthomas
CSM Ballroom	Clonea

Westmeath

County Arms Ballroom	Mullingar
Crescent Ballroom	Athlone
Greville Arms Hotel	Mullingar
Hodson Bay Hotel	Athlone
Roseland Ballroom	Moate

Royal Hotel	Athlone
Shamrock Lodge Hotel	Athlone
Lakeland Ballroom	Mullingar
Sportex Hall	Athlone
St Mary's Hall	Athlone
St Michael's Ballroom	Castlepollard

Wexford

Tara Ballroom	Courtown Harbour
Athenaeum Ballroom	Enniscorthy
Fern's Ballroom	Ferns
Hunt's Ballroom	Gorey
Castle Ballroom	Enniscorthy
Dun Mhuire	Wexford
Camross Ballroom	Wexford
Golf Hotel Ballroom	Rosslare

Wicklow

Arcadia Ballroom	Bray
International Hotel	Bray
Entertainment Centre	Arklow
Ormonde Ballroom	Arklow
Royal Hotel	Arklow
Arklow Bay Hotel	Arklow
Laurel Park Ballroom	Bray
Royal Hotel	Bray
La Touche Ballroom	Greystones
Enniskerry Ballroom	Enniskerry
Mall Ballroom	Wicklow
Bel Air Hotel	Ashford
Pavilion	Rathdrum
Scalp Ballroom	Enniskerry
Downshire Arms Hotel	Blessington

A constellation of stars. This rare photograph shows Ireland's leading showband frontmen. From left: Joe Dolan of the Drifters, Art Supple of the Victors, Dickie Rock of the Miami, Tom Dunphy of the Royal, Brendan Bowyer of the Royal (standing), Derek Deane of the Freshmen, Brendan O'Brien of the Dixies, Butch Moore of the Capitol; seated, front: Larry Cunningham of the Mighty Avons, Declan Ryan of the Regal and Tony Keeling of the Graduates.